# CAROLS OF CANADA, ETC., ETC.

# CAROLS OF CANADA, ETC., ETC.

## ELIZABETH S. MACLEOD

ISBN: 978-93-5614-635-8

Published: 1893

LECTOR HOUSE LLP
E-MAIL: info@lectorhouse.com

Sincerely yours
E. S. MacLeod

# CARLS OF CANADA, ETC., ETC.

BY

MRS. MACLEOD

1893

**TO**
**THE HONOURABLE**
**SIR DONALD A. SMITH,**
**K. C. M. G., LL. D.**

Who, with the more than regal right
Of generous heart, and princely hand
Hath fostered learning in our land;
And set it on the highest height.

Who faileth not 'fore certain test
Of faith supreme—true zeal for man;
Who, working out supernal plan,
Doth serve his God and country best,—

**THESE CAROLS OF CANADA, ETC., ETC.,**
**ARE**
**MOST RESPECTFULLY INSCRIBED.**

# PREFACE.

In sending forth these gleanings from the later compositions of my few leisure hours, I take the opportunity of thanking most sincerely those many friends who have so generously subscribed for the work. Not only has their kind appreciation caused me to realize that I am no longer a stranger in a strange land, but also, that I possess the whole-souled sympathy of not a few, in this the country of my adoption.

Many are the tender memories which unite me to the olden land: a land for ever hallowed as the quiet resting-place of the lovèd dead, and the once happy home of a love-encircled childhood. Still, I cannot but deplore the many evils existing therein; more especially that evil of a system which places the greater number at the mercy of the fewer—the debasing system of extensive landlordism; a system which may have suited in those former periods when kingdoms and positions were mainly dependent upon force of arms, but for which there can be no plausible apology in this progressive, and pretentiously humanizing age; and if any words of mine shall induce the tyrant-crushed and woe-oppressed of other climes to raise their eyes towards the setting sun, and to seek a home in this Canada,—this God-appointed haven, these words shall not have been penned in vain.

I cherish the utmost faith in the future of Canada—faith which leads me to look beyond my little day and view her, with ample resources still developing, with invitations of welcome still extended, a full-grown nation of intelligent, enterprising and generous-souled people, more glorious by far than the world-renowned empires of the past; a nation unfettered from bigotry of sect, envy of position, and clannishness of clime; a nation whose belief is in the eternal fatherhood of God, and the universal brotherhood of humanity; a nation whose every act of every day life is the pure and lofty exponent of a Christly Christianity, and in whose healthy moral atmosphere vice with its attendant train of evils cannot exist; a nation upon which, over all its boundless pasture lands and by its many sounding shores, the sun of Freedom shines, and the honest, earnest worshipper bendeth never a humble knee save to fair Freedom's God.

E. S. MACLEOD.

Charlottetown, Nov. 1893.

# CONTENTS

# CAROLS OF CANADA.

## CANADA.

Oh Canada! great Canada!
Land of all lands to be;
Farewell to lays of olden clime!
We touch the lyre for thee.
For thee, Oh gracious, morning land!
Through cycles of renown
Thy leal of heart, and firm of hand
Shall guard thy spotless crown.

Exhaustless, boundless Canada!
Thy myriad forests wave;
Thy snow-capped mountains cleave the skies;
Thy shores, two oceans lave.
Thy sea-wide lakes, thy rivers bold
Are worlds of crystal sheen;
And vast as empires famed of old
Thy prairies, rolling green.

Oh fair and beauteous Canada!
Aneath thy sapphire sky,
Gay-plumaged warblers wing their flight
O'er flowers of gorgeous dye,
Which own no faint, exotic blush
Of Care's trim, training hand;
Rich dowered of health, with nature's flush,
They brighten all the land.

Yet, not thy beauty, Canada,
Could hold thy people's love;
Yet not thy vastness, nor thy might
Could soul of nations move.
But this, that o'er thy gleaming lakes,
And through thy waving pines,
The glory of a future breaks;
The sun of freedom shines.

Thou may'st not boast, fair Canada!
The soft, spice-laden breeze;
Or palm of Ethiopian land,
Or pearl of Ceylon seas.
Yet thine no dread, samiel curse,
To blight thy emerald plains;
Thine only wholesome air, to nurse
Pure blood in patriot veins.

Thou may'st not point, young Canada!
To sumptuous mosques of pride;
Or watery highways, where with song,
The gay gondolas glide.
But thine, beneath wide starry dome,
Along ten thousand streams,
O'er many a league of richest loam,
To animate life dreams.

Thou opest, regal Canada!
Floodgates off either sea;
And tyrant-crushed, and crushed of fate,
Find peaceful rest in thee.
Upon thy generous-yielding sward,
And round thy teeming coast,
Just labor finds its just award;
Nor heart of hope is lost.

Oh high-souled! hopeful Canada!
Long may thy banner wave
O'er soil where will to work is gold,
Nor man nor mind is slave.
God's grace thee further, lovèd land!
Live thou thy high behest!
So shalt thou 'mid the nations stand
Erect; through blessing blest.

# SIEUR DE MAISONNEUVE, OR THE FOUNDING OF MONTREAL.

Tho' rough be the path thou art destined to tread,
Let courage and truth be thy stay;
Thy course be straight onward, aye looking ahead,
Doubt not, neither droop by the way.
Who spanned the wide ocean, who narrowed the soil,
With spirits untrammeled of fear,
Have found, through the struggle, the sorrow, the toil,
Sure help from on high ever near.

He had ta'en his last look of those terraced hills
Where the golden and green intertwine;
Where song of the peasant doth sing in the rills,
As he gleaneth the fruit of the vine.
He had breathed fond adieux to his own loved land,
A land of rare science and art;
Where learning's vast treasure to genius lends hand,
And knowledge ennobleth the heart.

Aglow with the fire of a heavenly grace,
He had sailed for the ice drift and snow;
With vigor of purpose had ventured his face
To yet fiercer, more deadly foe.
To the darkening scowl of the dusky crew
He would radiate beams of love;
Would labor and bide, with his well-chosen few,
The unction bestowed from above.

They told him of brothers who perished before;
Of the tortures of savage hate;
Vain pleading! it stirred but his courage the more
To conquer, or share in their fate.
Not his to recall, with a sigh of regret,
Those voices far over the main;
Where the sun of his brilliant boyhood set,
On the banks of the royal Seine.

Not his to feel faint on the thorniest path,
Or to shrink whate'er might betide:
They know not, or heed not humanity's wrath
Who are vowed to the Crucified.
He gazed on the shore, with its dark fringe of pine;
To the heavens, with bright disc on the blue;
Then, lightened his vision with rapture divine;
The future arose to his view.

"I shall go," said he, "unto Montreal
Though each tree were an Iroquois!"
And the God of the dauntless hearkened his call,
The God of the martyred ones saw.
Now the great city smiles where the grim forest loomed,
And the red man boweth the knee;
And the Cross which was trampled in triumph hath bloomed
From mountain to uttermost sea.

## THE HUNTSMAN.

'TWAS in the lone, uncultured wilds
Of far Assiniboia,
Ere commerce took its giant stride
From east to western sea.
From grasp of lordly tyranny
Came brave and sturdy band;
The sons of sires who framed the old,
To build the fair, new land.

The red men tracked the hunter's path
Through miles of gloomy wood;
And now, with whoop and fiendish yell,
Before their victim stood.
With rifle shot he kept his ground,
And held the foe at bay;
Yet, what avail his single strength!
Ten times his number they.

He leaped upon a rocky ledge
Which overhung the wave;
Far kindlier fate than scalping-knife,
The risk of watery grave.
He glanced towards his precious haven
Upon its patch of green;
He saw his loved ones by the door,
But—the river rolled between.

Another saw; love prompted wit;
Upon the grassy floor
She laid her babe, then fleetly sought
The wherry by the shore.
With strong, young arm she plied the oar;
The waters twirl and toss;
'Tis vain! beneath that cataract
No human power may cross.

List! through the noisome, seething surge,
A voice of hope and cheer:
"Leap in, and swim adown the stream,
I'll meet you—never fear!"

The current bears the slight skiff on,
The Indians' arrows fly,
But the huntsman's form is seen no more
Against that lurid sky.

For he hath plunged into the foam
And, borne upon the tide,
Is now beyond all chance of harm,
His brave wife by his side.
Saved by that faith-inspiring Love
Which glorifies the hearth;
Which amply fills with choice-drawn wealth,
And crowns the loves of earth.

# CAPE LE FORCE.

WHERE frowning bulwarks guard the coast
Around our sea-girt Isle,
Where wildest winters wreak their wrath,
And sweetest summers smile.

In holy calm of eventide
Which crowned the sunbright day,
We sat upon a grassy knoll
That overlooked the bay.

All glorious the lingering light
From out the radiant west,
As loath to leave a scene so fair,
Illumined ocean's crest.

Along the path, with quiet tread,
There came an aged form
Whose sunburnt features told that he
Had weathered many a storm.

He'd held command in goodly craft
On nigh and far off seas;
Had furled the sail on foreign strand,
And scoured 'fore every breeze.

Now, 'yond all lure of worldly wealth
Through commerce on the foam,
He anchored where affection set,
Within his childhood's home.

Nor tide, nor wind, nor black storm-cloud
Could bar his passage more,
As he waited sailing orders
For glad Beulah's shore.

We asked him, as he rested near,
If he the story knew
Of that bleak, lonely cape which stretched
Upon our right hand view.

"I can relate," he said, "the tale
My grandsire told to me:—
It happened in the year of grace

Seventeen sixty-three.

"That year the Isle of St. Jean
Was ceded, this you know,
To Britain, in the treaty signed
By France, at Fontainebleau.

"French privateers, which robbed our coast,
Were harassed by our men;
McKenzie, with a British sloop
Unaided, captured ten.

"One, fleeter than the rest escaped,
Commanded by Le Force;
In dread of foes, or unknown seas,
He held a leeward course.

"But all too fast the gallant ship
Bore down towards the bay;
Caught on deceitful shifting sands,
A stranded wreck she lay.

"The boats made shore, the crew dispersed,
One officer remained
With his commander, and large share
Of ill-won booty gained.

"On yonder cape they pitched a tent,
And from the vessel's store
In haste, with slightest interval,
Much precious freight they bore.

"But where 'twas hid no mortal knew;
Folk say within yon grove,
Whose crowding giants dull the day,
Exists the treasure-trove.

"Be't so or not, to me it seems
This cursed greed of gold
Shuts all the finer feelings out,
Deforms life's fairest mould.

"Rends rare affection's dearest ties,
Transforms the friend to foe;
In battlefield of worldly gain
Smites with unsparing blow.

"Repels all humanizing love;
In haste to reach its goal,
Draws even from gates of paradise
The earnest, God-ward soul.

"Two daring youths, from hamlet nigh,
Through motives curious, went
When friendly even lent its shades,
Anear the strangers' tent.

"They heard dispute o'er money hoard,
Then louder, wrathful tones,
Which hotter, higher, waxed until
They sunk in low, faint moans.

"Next morn three sturdy fishermen
Steered out across the wave;
They heeded not the swelling surge,
Their hearts were firm and brave.

"But, Oh! what vision met their gaze!
Upon that silent shore
The Captain of the stranded bark
Lay stiffening in his gore.

"Far from his loved in *La Belle France,*
Far from his native plain;
Where longing eyes, and yearning hearts
Might long for him in vain.

"He died not as the soldier dies;
For country and for king;
For him no martial banners wave,
No lyre his praise doth sing.

"Rough hands, but souls of sympathy,
Entombed him where he fell;
While sounding ocean wailed his dirge,
And wavelets rang his knell.

"Now, until ocean yields her dead,
Till dries yon river's source,
That cape, baptizèd with his blood,
Shall bear the name 'Le Force.'"

He paused. "What of the murderer?
And what to him befell?"
"He fled, from that dread hour of guilt
No tongue his fate could tell.

"No legal technicality
Could paint *his* black as white,
Or color with a golden tinge
The blackness of his night.

"Though richly-garbed, accomplished vice
May bide the Final Day;
With brutal, prompt, unstudied crime

The law brooks no delay.

"His was no deed of villain art
Which slowly works its will,
Which wiles its victim to his death,
And slays with callous skill.

"It may be that a Higher Judge
Could measure best his crime;
And that, through penitence he found
Pardon and peace in time."

The sun had sunk beneath the wave,
The moon had risen on high;
And glorified, with silvery beams,
The earth, and sea, and sky.

Light zephyrs thrilled on ocean's chords,
Through wavelet's hum and flow;
Alas! that scene surpassing fair,
Should sin or sorrow know.

Alas! that guilt, or causeless woe
Should darken nature's smile;
As that foul deed, the first to blight
With crime Prince Edward Isle.

# SISTER ST. THOMAS.

## I.

Bright beauty of northern winter!
The sun, with its tenderest glow,
Gilded the haze of the housetops,
Warm-tinted earth's mantle of snow.

Flashed forth the crystalline branches,
Bedazzling of jewelry rare;
Rich set in radiance of splendor,
Choice pearlets of nature's own wear.

Dark night with its gloom had faded,
Fair morning its halo unfurled;
Yet stirred not the solemn silence
With the hum of a waking world.

Unheard was the sound of labor,
Mute—hushed was the voice of the street;
Only the tread of passers by,
Who stayed not their hastening feet.

Only half whispers, curt replies
To eager questions, doubtful given;
For hearts were awed with sudden fear,
For dearest ties of earth were riven.

Soft cloudlets afloat on the blue,
Pure wreaths of the shimmering snow,
Re-uttered in language sublime,
The breathings of unwonted woe.

Alas, for the dreaming of life!
Though heard not the roll of the drum,
Nor witnessed the ensign of war,
A merciless tyrant had come.

Strife is no strife ill-divided
When man fighteth frail brother-man;
But war is a warfare unequal
When giant force leadeth one van.

What marvel that mortals shrank back,

That science e'en held bated breath;—
Over the lights of our dwellings
There hovered the angel of death.

The flags which drooped from the windows,
And waved in the winterly sun,
Signalled fierce battle was raging,
But told not of victory won.

They were no flags of our nation,
No tri-colored red, white and blue;
Heralds of hope, or of freedom,
Beamed not in their pale, saffron hue.

## II.

Inside the new oped lazar-house,
Where sick and dying, plague-struck, lay,
Skill sought to baffle foul disease,
Yet still the dismal blight made way.

Sore lack of helpful, nursing hands
Was keenly felt within those walls;
Since selfish dread had closed the soul
To lucre's bribe, or mercy's calls.

Had closed the soul of all save those
Whose life is but to do His will;
Who fear not Afric's burning sands,
Nor Javan swamp, nor Iceland chill.

Three Sisters, vowed to charity,
Out of the well trained city band;
Skilled nurses[1] they, and fit prepared,
Came forward as with life in hand.

When, shame to tell, their proffered aid
Was scouted; reason urgeth why?
Search not dim aisles of bigotry,
Sift thou thy soul for just reply.

Oh, narrow bounded prejudice!
Hedged round of a Christian name,
Thou low, dim burning altar light!
Unlit of celestial flame.

Right royal blood in honor's cause,

---

[1] "Skilled Nurses."—When the epidemic of small-pox visited Charlottetown in the year 1885, three nuns from the City Hospital volunteered their professional services. The generous offer was at first refused, but afterwards gladly accepted. Sister St. Thomas never recovered from the effects of her labours in the improvised Hospital; she died in Montreal the following Spring.

Red stains the patriot battle field;
Thou slay'st thy myriads for naught,
God in the conscience may not yield.

Thou! blind and selfish prejudice;
Vile, murky source of endless strife;
Know that a world reviving faith
Doth blossom into fruitful life.

## III.

Still raged the dreaded pestilence,
And still the quiet stars of night
Beamed down upon the obsequies
Of those who perished in the fight.

'Mid comfort of our peaceful homes,
We heard the rattle of the car
Which bore the vanquished from the scene
Of bloodless, but relentless war.

For them no sacred bell was tolled,
Nor rose the chant of plaintive psalm;
Yet through deep mists shone guiding light
From cruel cross, to blissful palm.

Within the City Hospital,
With satchel in her willing hand,
She waited, as a soldier waits,
Intent to hear his lord's command.

She knew that fickle human aid
When sought at risks is sought in vain;
That in no human breast exists
Will to encounter death or pain.

"And can'st thou think to go?" I said,
"When all thy purposes of good
Were balked by callous ignorance,
Close-linked with base ingratitude."

She looked me calmly in the face;
A shade, which noted sad surprise
Stole o'er her placid countenance,
And spake from out her gentle eyes.

Her answer echoes down the years,
Illumes the hall in which she sat,
Breaks through all cant of class or creed:—
*"Those sick must not suffer for that.."*

## IV.

Just then a messenger was hailed;
To God and to their mission true,
Firm-souled, went out to meet the plague
She and devoted sisters two.

Emblazoned in archives of light
Those titles no worldling may hold;
Whilst their star, in our nether sky,
Shines forth in a circlet of gold.

With practised eye, and tender hand,
With quiet mien, and noiseless tread,
They grappled with the dire disease,
Or soothed the sufferer's dying bed.

They listed, with a patient mind,
The longings of the exiled one;
Or treasured, for a mother's ear,
The last faint accents of her son.

Yea! all along that tardy night,
Black with the bitterness of woe,
They toiled in unison with those
Whose skill and courage[2] foiled the foe.

Fame proudly vaunts her hero dead;
Ambition's tools, in glory's van;
Thrice worthy he of lasting wreath,
Who lives for God, and dies for man.

Ah me! for the silent martyr
Whose tireless feet so surely trod
The pathway leading on and up
Towards the city of our God.

The poison draught entered her blood;
In brightness of Spring's early day
Sister St. Thomas bowed her head,
And passed from her labors for aye.

I know that 'yond the swelling surge,
She reached that tideless, tranquil shore,
Where faith finds anchor nigh its source,
And storms of time are heard no more.

---

[2] "Whose skill and courage."—Dr. Richard Johnson, Health Officer, distinguished himself by unremitting devotion to his arduous duties; and also, along with Dr. Warburton, attended all cases in the city; while Dr. J. T. Jenkins, with his son, Dr. S.R. Jenkins, were in constant attendance at the Hospital. Notable also were Mayor H. Beer, and clergymen Carruthers, O'Meara and MacIntyre.

I know that robed in spotless white,
Her pure soul on Mount Zion stands;
And yet I see her as she sat
With satchel in her willing hands.

Ho, peerless crown! Ho, fadeless palm!
Bright land where ransomed spirits be!
True love to God with love to man,
Ensures a blessed eternity.

## THE MESSAGE.

Ye sweet summer birds! in your flight
Afar o'er the southern sea,
Will ye stoop from your aerified height
To whisper my lover of me?

Again will ye hoist your bright wing
When ice-fields unloose from our shore;
New tunes through the woodlands shall ring;—
Those tones! shall I hear never more?

Remind him that low in the sky
Sails the god of the long summer day;
That later the glory-glints hie
From their couch, with its curtains of gray.

Yet—tell him through nature's vast range,
Reaped harvests, ripe forests aflame;—
Oh! tell him, through oceans of change,
I'll love him forever, the same.

# HIS OFFERING.

"WHERE's mother?" and with eager haste
He bore Love's offering;
The first, bright flowers which oped their eyes;
Sweet heralds of the Spring.

Those tiny stars which dot with light
The young year's tender green;
As silvery tapers gem the doole
Of evening's sable screen.

Ho! worlding of the callous mind!
Deem this a trifling thing?
O'er little deeds of loyal love
Great mother-love doth sing.

More precious from those chubby hands,
Those sweet, wild flowers of Spring,
Than priceless jewels from the store
Of coroneted king.

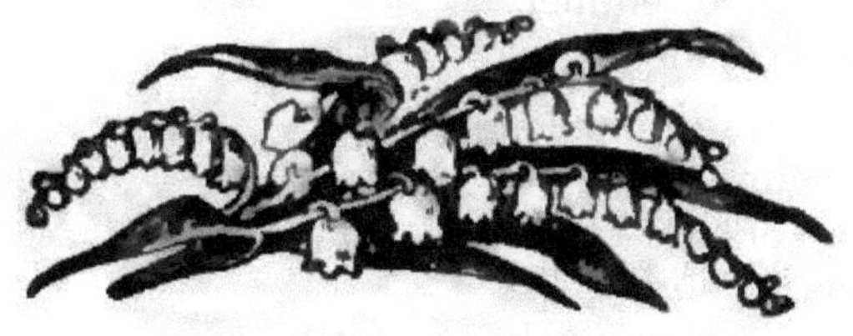

# LOUISBURG—1745.

"Unbridled appetite was followed by deadly fever, and before Spring 1200 of Peperell's men filled graves in the conquered soil."

Brave maiden-love! bright sister-faith!
Of this Columbian land,
Why should fair youth, as tidal wreck,
Drift up on either strand?
Ye mothers! when your sons set sail
On life's tempestuous seas,
Why pray ye Heaven's propitious calm
To quell each rising breeze?

If haste for fame, or wealth of lore,
Or thirst for worldly pelf
Be set above that priceless boon,
The power to conquer self.
To guard that no insidious foe
The citadel shall win;
To note, as quick-eared sentinel,
The first approach of sin.

The surges tossed in seething foam
Upon that rock-bound shore;
Yet the brave men of New England
Down to the leeward bore.
The Frenchman's warning gun booms forth,
The heavy seas resound;
What reck they! with determined mien
They tread the solid ground.

Mere raw recruits and all untrained
In stratagem of war,
Not Gallia's veterans, skilled in arms,
Their landing place might bar.
Through hardships dire and manifold
They upward, onward press;
On, till the blossomings of hope
Are fruited with success.

And all through proud New England,
And far across the wave,
The name of Massachusetts
And of her soldier brave
Is linked with joy and feasting;
While Britain's fair renown
Gleams fairer for the added gem,
Which decks her ancient crown.

More bright the clear, translucent sky,
More dense the shadows fall;
More glorious the spirits glow,
More black the dismal pall;
Oft, through celestial sunlight,
Breaks forth dull thunder shower;
Oft, over brilliant visionings
Dark disappointments lower.

So, in first flush of triumph,
Crept in an artful foe,
Whose craft and daring overcame
Without one open blow.
More certain than the Gascon shot
In siege, on field of war;
And deadlier than the scalping knife
Of subtle Indian, far.

And those brave, who never faltered
Before a human form,
Who never shrank from danger's path,
Or cowered beneath a storm,
Fall down before that reaper's hand
As falls the sun scorched grain;
And Glory's wreath, and Victory's song
Alike are void and vain.

# THE WOODS AND THE SEA.

THEY gathered round with feeling heart,
From hamlet far and near;
They strove in vain, with kindly words,
Her stricken soul to cheer.
For over the night of anguish
Dawned never break of day;
That sun which sank in frowning skies
Left ne'er a softening ray.

Oh broken heart! Oh empty life!
Oh sad, low monotone!
"The woods and the sea have ruined me;
Alone! yea all alone!"

She'd left her peaceful, native shores
And dared the stormy wave
With him whose troth was love and truth;
The young, the strong and brave.
They raised a cabin on the wild,
In shade of branching tree;
And there the mother reared the child,
And time passed merrily.

Toil reaped the gain of comfort sweet;
And by the fireside blaze,
Glad souls went up in grateful song,
In voice of joy and praise.
Sweet lyrics of the heather land
The evening hours beguiled;
While age re-lived its youth once more,
And happy childhood smiled.

Dark shadows mar the brightest heaven,
And, sharp as warning bell,
Sore tidings of their sailor's death
Upon that homestead fell.
Then, when the winter spread earth's shroud
Of pure white, glistening snow,
Upon those mourners fell apace
A still more bitter blow.

All night, amid the biting frost,
With darkest gloom o'er head,
Upon the fir-tree's broken boughs
Three wanderers made their bed.
But, ere the dawn had streaked the sky
With glorious hues of day,
The brightest life e'er blessed a home
Was stilled in death for aye.

The seasons cycled; peaceful years
Again verged into woe;
By fatal stroke of falling tree
The silvered head lay low.
She stood beside the aged form;
Her brain seemed all on fire;—
The billows rolled, the forest waved
O'er fated sons and sire.

Oh narrow bounds of earthly ill!
Oh sad and suffering throng!
Oh ye! who drink the bitter cup;
It cannot be for long.
The woe-worn frame now resteth well;
The soul hath found its own;
Where shades of earth no more may blight,
In lustre of the Throne.

No more she sings, in lonely grief
Her weary monotone:
"The woods and the sea have ruined me;
Alone! yea, all alone!"

# THE GATE.

## I

THE light of love o'er her features played,
The silver streaks through her bright hair strayed.

Her noble mien and her gentle hand
Proclaimed her daughter of no mean land.

Voice and action attested her birth,
Better than mere gilt baubles of earth.

Winter had folded its shroud and fled;
The daisies peeped from their grassy bed.

The dark mounds rose from their circling green;
Young plants smiled back to the bright'ning sheen.

No wealth of splendor, yet choice as gold
Those gifts from hands of the loved of old.

Hands which will clasp my hand nevermore
Till feet stand firm on the tideless shore.

Careless young Playful had oped the gate;
Hastening footsteps, that could not wait,

Had sped where playtime and boyhood meet;
The gate, forgot, swung ope from the street,

From the highway where the cattle roam,
And Arabs find their kindliest home.

The gate might swing till the twilight hours;
Meantime, alack for the tender flowers!

## II.

Came she, 'mid the many passers by;
Quick of the wit and clear of the eye.

She, of the high-bred, Christian school,
Soul-lit and sunned of the golden rule.

Questioned she whether! halted she long!
Qualms of propriety right no wrong.

Yield form and fashion their fitting place;
Yet, cramp not the soul in meaner space.

Hence to marauders, and riskings of fate,
She quietly closed—then latched the gate.

Trumpet bequests of the miser-mind,
Who spreads abroad when he cannot bind.

Boast ye those deeds which blazon the name,
Lofty as adamant heights of Fame.

Dawning of glory! the world's great heart
Throbs not its truest response to art.

Nor skill, nor fame, nor glamour of gold;
Only Love's chain doth the world enfold.

And those who will soar on angel wings,
Are the generous even in smaller things.

Generous when shadows darken fate,
To close 'gainst evil a neighbor's gate.

# THE HIDING PLACE.[3]

The low, sweet voice of a summer's sea
Floats far along the pebbly strand;
Whilst melodies, from greening grove,
Resound o'er all the pleasant land.
The streamlet, freed from icy band,
Sings gaily on its seaward way;
All nature, in responsive mood,
Doth chime in Springtide roundelay.

What notes discordant dare to mar
Those tender cadenzas of song?
Can those shrill tones be tones of wrath
On softest zephyrs borne along?
Yea! over Ocean's peaceful hum
A woman's wrathful voice soars high;
And through the green-arched forest aisles
Rings out young childhood's plaintive cry.

Who cometh, arrayed in priestly guise,
Full-charged with embassy divine,
Of noble mien, of princely port,
Of lofty brow and look benign?
The mother stays the uplifted hand;—
The culprit turned, and quickly ran
And refuge sought, and shelter found
Beneath cloak of the holy man.

Calm, clear and firm the warning fell
"Forgive! if thou wouldst be forgiven;
Whose heart doth harbor angry thoughts
Can ne'er as penitent be shriven.
Forgive thy son! this once forgive!
His surety I shall gladly be;
Or, if justice claimeth punishment,
Then—visit his crimes on me."

* * * * *

[3] "The Hiding-place."—Incidents in the career of the much beloved and widely lamented Bishop MacIntyre.

The years rolled on; the priestly garb
Bedecks a princely prelate now;
The saintly voice a blessing speaks
From underneath a mitred brow.
In his rounds of zeal the Bishop seeks
Once more fair Lennox' sea-girt isle;
When lo! from out the gathering shades,
The brilliant lights of welcome smile.

In centre of a glittering throng
The reverend Father stately stands;
And, in the name of the Triune God,
He upraiseth his sacred hands.
Whilst, leader in that vast array,
Whose torches brighten wave and shore,
Is he whose faults were answered for;
The saved of many years before.

So we, in our rebel sin-nature,
Pine under the chastening rod;
And fly with our burden of evil
From wrath of a just-dealing God,
To hide in Christ's sheltering raiment
Of righteousness, inwove with peace;
To find, in a sinless substitute,
The sin-fettered soul's release.

So we, when our Great High Priest shall come,
Begirt of power, enrobed of state,
And the peoples of ten thousand isles
With eager joy His advent wait,
Shall hail, with a heartsong of rapture,
His step on our sin-furrowed strand;
Shall march, with the grand triumphal throng,
In the glow of a God-lit land.

# A CHRISTMAS MEMORY.

Hail Christmas! beacon ever bright;
Athwart the way-worn years;
Full lustred of celestial light,
Thy white-robed dawn appears.
Blest season! when our much beloved
Around one altar meet;
When voices from the spirit-land
Our longing spirits greet.

In tender memories arise,
Sunlit, the days of old,
When radiant vistas oped the skies
And streaked earth's grey with gold.
Beneath a lofty castle dome
Three fair young dreamers smile;
And, fraught of love, the light of home,
The flitting hours beguile.

They wander by the river side,
They rest in woodland bowers;
Pure joy flows like the rippling tide
Through all the sunny hours.
They climb the purple mountain crest,
They list the vesper call;—
Ah me! gay life, then quiet rest;
Earth's shadows! darksome pall!

Yet, lo! seraphic vision breaks;—
That beauteous band I see,
Where glory-dawn in gladness wakes;
Where all the ransomed be.
High-seated in Immanuel's land,
'Yond shadow of the tomb;
Safe-nurtured 'neath a Father's hand
Immortal youth doth bloom.

Oh! happy, happy hearted!
Who tread the golden floor;
Oh! sinless, early parted!
Who live, to die no more.

Bright land, where none may sever!
Where life is life for aye;
Where, through the long forever,
No night shall veil the day.

Within the grand, orchestral throng
They harp, with crownèd brow;
While sadness mingles with our song,
We at His footstool bow.
Hail Christmas! light to weary eyes!
Light thou the years along;
Till, all as one in Paradise,
We sing our Christmas song.

## THE IMMIGRANT'S APPEAL.

Oh! ye who suffer ills untold
Upon the ground you tread!
Whose children pine from want and cold,
And cry in vain for bread,
Fold not your hands o'er cruel fate,
Nor weep with blinded eyes;
Look onward! peace and plenty wait
Aneath our western skies.

I left my home in Erin's Isle,
By Shannon's glittering wave,
I bade farewell a mother's smile,
A youthful husband's grave.
Together with my orphan band
I crossed the raging sea,
And sought and found in this bright land
A home for them and me.

Where riches may not rob the feast
Won by the hand of toil;
Nor oust the man to feed the beast
Upon God's fertile soil.
Where sterling worth may upright stand,
Where industry is blessed;—
Yes! though I love my native land,
I love this land the best.

Here Scotia finds her sweet blue bell,
Here Erin's shamrock blows;
Whilst incense floats o'er hill and dell
From England's fragrant rose.
Each country finds its own again
Tenfold, in this great world,
Where Freedom's hand, from mount to main,
Her banner hath unfurled.

Fair Canada! all lands above
In power to conquer wrong;
Thou yieldest love in turn for love,
Thy strength shall aye be strong.

Oh beauteous, peerless, wide domains!
Oh ever teeming store!
Though exiled myriads seek thy plains,
There's room for myriads more.

Now, where the Rocky summits rise,
At tender eve's decline,
I watch the sun of cloudless skies
O'er many an acre shine.
My heart's best treasures by my side,
The years may ebb and flow;
Till I shall greet, 'yond storm and tide,
The loved of long ago.

## THE QUEEN'S JUBILEE.

### I.

Ring out, gay notes! through the brightening blue;
Peal forth o'er the shimmering wave;
Re-echo in souls of the brave;
Bestir the hearts of the loyal and true.

Waft the sweet strains from the dear Mother-land
To the dwellers by far off sea;
Loud anthem the glad Jubilee
From white-robed North unto burnished strand.

Anthem the years of the peaceful decades
When learning asserted its sway,
And poortith revived in its ray;
When science and art illumined our glades.

Broken that power which the conscience would bind,
Base umpire 'twixt God and the soul;
No tyrant free speech doth control;
Loosed are the fetters which burdened the mind.

Rides Progress aloft on triumphal car,
Out-coursing the wings of the wind;
To the gorgeous fanes of Ind
Rich blossoms his path, from the Polar star.

Philanthrophy opeth her gentle hand;
Devotion Heaven's dictate obeys;
Dawns clearly Hope's halcyon days;—
Golden their gleam, as Aurora's bright wand.

Live Commerce, careering the white crested wave,
Quells baneful suspicion and fear;
From high unto lowliest sphere
Blendeth in union—our Empire to save.

### II.

Now harmony striketh a tender chord
In the lay true Loyalty sings;
For the offering which she brings

Is dearer than trophy won by the sword.

Praise for those virtues which never wax old,
Lustrous gems in a noble life;
Praise for the calm amid the strife;—
Serene is the spirit of sterling gold.

Rolls from our vision the mist of the years,
Adown through the dark aisles of time,
Life's canvas, with picture sublime,
In its radiance of beauty, appears.

Soft falleth the sun of a kindly zone
On the Abbey, so old and grey;
On the tomb of a former day;
Bathing in splendor the image of stone.

Sparkling in flame on the jewelled brow
Of the peeress, highborn and fair;
Anon on the mouldering chair,
Yclad of the royal, pure ermine, now.

Arrayed in the trappings of princely state,
Loadstar of a glittering band;
Our fair young Lady of the land—
She stands—the greatest where all are great.

Crowned with the crown which her brave fathers bore,
Largess of honors kiss her feet;
Enwraps her with dignity meet
Prestige of might, as the birthright of yore.

High-throned in the love of a nation's heart,
Rich treasures of promise, I ween,
Cheer the steps of our youthful Queen;
Lighten the future, and courage impart.

## III.

Vanished that picture of glorious youth,
Dark clouds o'er life's midsummer came;
Yet scathless the seasons retain
The loving trust, and the honor and truth.

Full oft, o'er the fairest spring morning,
There falleth a bitter, cold blight;
Oft shroudeth in darksomest night
The ruddiest sun heaven adorning.

So fell *he* in full flush of his manhood,
So dropt *they* in life's glowing spring;
Yet the anguished soul wakened to sing,

The tear-bedimmed eyes perceived the All-Good.

Richer than diamond of Indian mine
The treasure Victoria owns;
Firmest pillar of earthly thrones,
True sympathy,—typing the Love Divine.

Thrice blessèd sympathy! may it surround
And cheer her graceful evening's calm;
Till sceptre yields to victor's palm,
May the faith and hope, and the love abound.

Voice then the homage of millions as one;
Wreathe garlands of amaranth flowers;
Nor last be Canada—hers and ours;—
For here doth the blood of true fealty run.

Thunder it over the wide ocean's sheen!
Sing it by peaceful inland sea;
"God bless our glorious Jubilee!
God bless and defend our most noble Queen!"

# POINT PRIM.

Far off from the smoke, and the city's glare,
To the breath of the clover lea;
From the din and dust to the healthful air,
And the song of a tranquil sea.
Which falls on the ear like a holy psalm
From a world unkenned of strife;
As the eve glides past in a blissful calm,
Like the close of a well-spent life.

Yet sighings of sorrow are heard in the foam
Which white-wreathes thy border, Point Prim;
As she telleth their fate, who left thee, to roam,
The eyes of the mother wax dim.
Of him who ne'er quitted dread danger's post
Till engulfed in the treacherous wave;
Or of him who fevered on sultry coast,
And was launched in the sailor's grave.

No thrilling oration shall vaunt their praise,
No flowers bloom over their breast;
The surges shall wail through the long, long days,
Yet disturb not their quiet rest.
No kindred shall bind them in narrow bed,
No marble earth's sympathy crave;
Sea-shells will pillow the wave-shrouded head,
And winds sigh the dirge of her brave.

No more by the wood path, through falling leaves,
Will she hasten their steps to greet;
But yet will she gather her golden sheaves,
When time and eternity meet.
No more will they weather the tempest's strain,
With a lowering sky o'erhead;—
One haven will shelter her loved again
When the sea giveth up its dead.

# ORWELL BAY.

Sweet, pale-faced Queen of silent night!
Calm-seated on thy azure throne,
Shed forth thy beams of silvery light
Till nether realms embrace thine own.
Till gleaming spire on tree-crowned hill,
With waving corn on valley land;
Till peaceful flood, and noiseless mill
Seem burnished of enchanter's wand.

And you, ye moonbeams! softly glide
Along fair Orwell's glittering wave;
And gently rest where all my pride
Lies buried, in my Mary's grave.
Oh Mary! lovèd of my youth!
Oh blissful dreams of early day!
When love was life, and troth was truth,
And hallowed shrine was Orwell Bay.

Full oft, upon thy banks, of yore,
With hearts entwined in love divine,
While murmuring wavelets kissed thy shore,
We watched the radiant day's decline.
When sorrow fell, when times were hard,
Love held its faith, youth hoped the best;
I bade farewell thy greening sward,
And turned me to the glowing West.

Dull seasons fled, dark shadows lowered,
My utmost efforts were unmeet;
When sudden, fickle Fortune showered
Her golden largess at my feet.
As needle turneth to the pole,
So, homeward hied my steps to thee;
But ne'er shall love, or kindred soul,
Or joys of youth return to me.

Not all my wealth of hard-won gold
Could shield from blight that lustrous head
Now lying in the churchyard mould;—
The church where we had hoped to wed.

I list the sweet, clear notes which thrill
Through wooded uplands o'er thy wave;
The music in my heart is still,
Still as the stars o'er Mary's grave.

Oh, gorgeous lamps of living light!
Which halo all the arc of blue,
Ye emblem to my raptured sight
The white soul of a life most true.
My Mary! tender guiding star!
I bow before the Sovereign sway;—
That higher realm, where nought can mar,
Is fairer e'en than Orwell Bay.

## GOING ABROAD.

Oh fleeting hour! Oh faltering heart!
Oh long and sad farewell!
How bitter long we twain may part
It is not ours to tell.
For many a golden shaft will beam
Through many a pearly rain,
Down forest aisles, o'er mountain stream,
Ere we can meet again.

Yet, when on far off ocean's foam,
Or on some foreign strand,
Bright Memory wafts thy spirit home
Unto thy native land,
Bethink thee of those gladsome days
When carelessly we strayed
O'er furrowed sand, or daisied braes,
While Ocean minstrels played.

'Neath gleaming skies of cloudless blue;
Beyond the tropic's glare,
Where bright-eyed birds of rainbow hue
Float through the perfumed air;
By pictured scenes of former age;
In seats of ancient lore,
Where poet, painter, sculptor, sage
Illumined days of yore,

Recall that grand, familiar sight,
When heaven seems all ablaze
With floods of gold and purple light,—
Aurora's matchless rays.
And when, from black, dissonant sky
No stars may vigil keep;
When boisterous seas exult on high
And o'er the taffrail sweep,

Bethink thee of those days to be,
When floods shall swell no more;
Nor loud-voiced surge, nor angry sea
Shall break upon the shore.

Where white-winged storm shall never beat
Across the verdant plain;
Where severed lives, once more complete,
E'erlasting life shall gain.

# THE STUDENT.

THE cloudless sun of southern clime
Shone full that Christmas Day,
As the city of the Cæsars
Held regal holiday.

For Him whose gracious advent,
Hailed in seraphic tone,
The saved of earth, and saints in Heaven
In grateful praises own.

Full loud above the city's hum
Pealed forth cathedral chime;
While round the loftiest, proudest dome,
Wreathed harmony sublime,

Which thrilled among those ruins vast
That long have braved the skies;
Proud monument of Pagan hate
And Christian sacrifice.

Rejoicing echoes filled the breeze
That fanned the martyrs' tombs;
Fit requiem! they sowed the seed
Which now triumphant blooms.

Where Reason held its vaunted sway,
Firm-leagued with Godless might,
Round storied urn, through marbled halls
Loud shriek the birds of night.

Whilst borne along the sounding waves
Which fleck the furthest shore,
That light of life, that perfect faith
Sealed with the martyrs' gore.

But, within that regal city,
On that bright Christmas Day,
In hectic flush of fever heat
A stranger student lay.

A stranger from a distant land
Across the western sea,
Where peace doth reign, and howe'er poor

Man feels that he is free.

Of faith inspired, he'd crossed the foam
And left his native sod,
That he his years might consecrate
To winning souls for God.

No higher aim was ever sought,
No purer soul was shriven;
For the whole purpose of his life
Unto his Lord was given.

A noble matron sat beside
And soothed his dying bed;
One who, with mother's tenderness,
Had wept *her* early dead.

Sore, sore it grieved that mother's heart!
When fever's pulse beat high
And reason reeled, the parchèd lips
Gave forth the wailing cry,

"Oh! take me to that far-off land
Where cool sea-breezes blow;
Where wintry sun doth smiling shine
Athwart the pure, white snow.

"Oh! thither wist I to return
Fraught with my mission high,
To bear the standard of the Cross
Beneath my native sky.

"For this my spirit waked to zeal
Where soft the sunlight falls;
For this I craved the higher lore
Of Propaganda's halls."

Then "list the strains of music!
Now loud, now soft and clear;—
It is the voice of wavelets sweet
Which greets my listening ear.

"Brimful of glee, it seems to me,
They ripple o'er the strand,
As when they sang the lullaby
Of our dear, household band.

"Mark how the lustrous, Autumn glow
Illumes the reddening leaves;
The genial harvest-tide is past,
And gathered in, the sheaves.

"Now there—yes! through the waning light
I see the little stile;—
A few steps more—how dark it grows!
Home in Prince Edward Isle."

But as, o'er the calm of evening
Breathed forth the vesper hymn,
The visions of fancy faded,
The clear, blue eyes waxed dim.

The hectic flush evanished
Before cold Pallor's hand;
Ended the warfare, hushed the voice—
Hushed in the silent land.

And the soul of the fair young dreamer
Went up with music's swell;
Whilst Victory's pæans grandly soared
High o'er earth's parting knell.

And though to his home and kindred
He cometh ne'er again,
The memory of his bright young life
The years will aye retain.

And aye, as the festive season falls,
On fair St. Lawrence Bay,
They mourn the student who died in Rome
On that bright Christmas Day.

## THE PIONEER.

He sat 'neath the green verandah shade at cool of a sunbright day;
And many a pleasant look he cast to the children at their play.

Though blanched his locks, though stooped his form, his heart no frosts might sere,
For peacefully the shadows fall, where mind and soul are clear.

At length the noisy mirth is hushed for breathing space of rest,
And gaily round the loved grandsire the merry group hath pressed.

There's gentle Effie, little Will, big Joe and sturdy Ben,
Grandpa's namesake, "who sure will make his mark 'mongst mighty men."

"A story!" and the spectacles are moved from off the face,
And carefully and kindly wiped ere slipped into their case.

"A story! well, it seems to me that all my tales are told;
Both of these nigh, fast fleeting years, and long, long days of old."

Upwafted from the clover field, in fragrance on the wind,
Came breathings from a former hour in freshness to the mind.

"Perchance you have not listed how one stroke from woman's hand
Transformed a forest dense and dim to fair and fruitful land.

"'Twas in a far back settlement, within a dusky wood,
The rude hut of an immigrant on scanty clearance stood.

"Strong hands had reared the rooftree, and sowed the patch of ground,
And bleating from the sheepfold broke the solitude around.

"From rim of rudely builded flue the hazy smoke-wreaths curled,
To wander o'er the mighty vault which guards a sleeping world.

"Out of the widely opened door doth savory flavor steal
As, from gun of clever marksman, is prepared the evening meal.

"Beside the woodpile, which was hauled across last winter's snow,
Sat the owner of the homestead, but his head was bending low.

"He had flung aside his hatchet and tired and care-oppressed,
Sat down to muse and vex his mind, while he gave his body rest.

"His heart yearned o'er the byegone hours, on Scotia's bonny braes,
When he chased among the yellow broom, or plucked the juicy slaes.

"He hears the plashing of the wave upon the sea-beat shore;
He hears his mother's gentle step, as music on the floor.

"He sees the ivy-mantled church on yonder green hill side
Where, in his earlier manhood, he claimed his girlish bride.

"But the past is passed forever, and in its place doth stand
The certain fate of pioneer in our Canadian land.

"A match 'twixt strength of arm and will, of labor tough and keen,
Affording slightest intervals for idleness, I ween,

"And nature in repellant mood; in roughest, homeliest guise;
Of frowning features, fit to thwart the purpose from the prize.

"He conjured up his hardships in this new land of the West,
And reasoned of returning to the land he loved the best.

"But within the cot was wanted fresh fuel for the flame;
Impatient to the woodstack a trim young matron came.

"She steadied with her nimble foot the log late split in twain;
She raised the axe, but action failed; her stroke descends in vain.

"It failed, yet failed not; it had touched one sad, desponding heart,
And nerved his arm and urged him on to act the manlier part.

"Shame mantled o'er his sunbrowned cheek, and tinged his yet fair brow;
The mists fell from his longing eyes; he faced the real now.

"He looked unto the forest with its miles of birch and pine,
Its maple, and its tangled growth through which no sun might shine.

"He looked unto the forest with its giants great and tall;
He looked unto the forest but—God ruleth over all.

* * * * *

"Through years of active industry, through perfect trust in Heaven,
'Yond all the ups and downs of life complete success was given.

"I, for I was that laggard, by that stroke of woman's hand,
Was started on the royal road which needs no wizard wand.

"We planned and worked together—my Effie dear and I,
And quickly o'er our busy life the sunny years went by.

"For denseness of the solemn pine, came cheerful apple bloom;
And gleeful shouts of buoyant hearts outrang the sighs of gloom.

"For screeching owl, and croaking frog, came lowing of the cows,
As the merry bells went jingle, beyond the ample mows.

"Our boys grew up to help us; our boys—their mother's pride;
And ne'er a cloud came o'er our joys until our first-born died.

"A village sprung up near the farm; steam engines whistled by;
And the dusky serpent trailed its fumes along our placid sky.

"Then your father brought a fair young wife, our waning hours to cheer;
Her face was sweet as daffodil, her voice as song-bird's clear.

"But one morn there came a message,—Joe! you remember all;
And grandma heard it cheerfully, and answered to the call.

"My love! who loved me ever, from morn till gloaming grey,
Dear heart! who never murmured o'er the home of early day.

"For though she loved the olden land with love that knew no change,
With fuller life her sympathies found freer, broader range.

"The kind eyes closed, the busy hands were crossed on silent breast;
And reverently her mourning sons conveyed her to her rest.

"Beside her first-born on the hill—and there I hope to lie
When the blessed Lord doth summon me to meet her in the sky."

He looked upon the tasseled corn, the richest crop all round,
Then wistfully he gazed beyond to the now hallowed ground

Where slept his past; he faintly sighed, then bowed his agèd head;—
The children strove to rouse him but—the loved grandsire was dead.

No more he tells of struggle vast, or rest from labour won;
He singeth in the psalms of peace 'neath an unsetting sun.

No more he sees with vision dim; upon that other shore
The Light of Life hath welcomed him to glory evermore.

# THE OLDEN FLAG.

Raise high the royal standard!
Shame not thy royal birth;
The prestige of thy might sustain,
Thou noblest of the earth!
Great Canada! thou fair, free land!
A world looks forth to thee;
No alien hand thy hand shall lead;
Thou'lt bow no servile knee.

Then rally round the olden flag!
The loved red, white and blue;
Let traitors scheme, or boasters brag,
To Canada prove true.

Float on, Oh flag of Empire vast!
Long may thy colors wave
O'er many a blood-bought heritage;
O'er many a hero's grave.
The grandeur of thy fame doth light
The fields our fathers won;
The noblest gift which valiant sire
Could e'er bequeath his son.

Droop not, Oh peerless standard!
Oh loyal hearts and true!
Forget not ye the olden land
Though cherishing the new.
Forget not hearts and hopes are one,
From Britain's sea-girt Isles
To where, beyond the Rocky steep,
The broad Pacific smiles.

Wave on, Oh flag of Empire vast!
O'er mountain, rock and stream;
Where wholesome fealty rests secure,
Beneath thy fervent gleam.
For, should the tramp of hostile feet
Arouse our peaceful shore,
Britannia's conquering sword would flash
Through Canada once more.

Then rally round the olden flag!
The loved red, white and blue;
Let traitors scheme, or boasters brag,
To Canada prove true.

# IDYLLS OF THE YEAR.

# THE OLD YEAR AND THE NEW.

## THE OLD.

We hailed thy white-robed natal hour,
Rejoiced in dawning Spring;
Now Autumn fruit, and Summer flower
Have passed, and sad we sing

Thy requiem. Oh vanished year!
Thy deeds of shame and wrong,
Thy widows' cry, thy orphans' tear
Well nigh untune my song.

Thine was the fraud, the private cheat,
The mean in purse and thought;
Leal worshippers at Mammon's feet,
Who sold their Heaven for nought.

Thine were those souls that slander hatch,
That tortuous tangles spin;
Who mimic those they fail to match,
And mock at all, save sin.

Thine too, those hideous slaughter-fields
Where, on the sodden plain,
As mind in man to brute force yields,
Lie dead, and deathless slain.

Yet, through that Power who quelled the storm
With mandate "Peace! be still!"
Thy friendships were not all mere form,
Thy doings not all ill.

For earnest hearts, and righteous hands
In thee have gained a prize,
That goal which change and time withstands;
Christ-life the world defies.

Then, blessing Him whose presence flows
Where vision fails to view;

Through summer's heat, and winter's snows,
We bid thee, Year, adieu!

## THE NEW.

And turn, with heart of hope, to hail
God's gift, the latest born;
Those promises which never fail
Make glad our New Year's morn.

Before His fiat nature bends,
His verdure clothes the tree;
He grandeur to the mountain lends,
And sways the surging sea.

At His command the torrents pour,
The spring leaps from the rock;
The eaglets from the eyrie soar,
Firm earth sustains a shock.

With power unbounded at His feet
All heaven and earth to move;
Through Calvary's cross, in Him we greet,
'Yond justice, pardoning love.

Though dismal clouds at noontide lower,
What need to grope our way;
Ahead doth stream, from beacon tower,
Light to celestial day.

That Hand which paints the rose's bloom,
Which hung heaven's canopy,
Doth point to where, 'yond present gloom,
Unblemished landscapes be.

That Heart, responsive to the cry
Of man, and bird, and beast;
Bids teeming earth, in prompt reply,
Spread out perpetual feast.

Then, sigh not o'er the buried year,
Nor mourn, in low-set voice;
Young Life sings forth in accents clear;
In her sweet joy rejoice.

## SPRING.

THE fiat hath gone forth;
From Winter's nerveless grasp
The frozen chains unclasp;
King Freedom rules our North.

From out his long repose
Fair Ocean sings again;
Low wail, or sweet refrain
In every breeze that blows.

See! from the listening hills
The whitened mantle glides;
Whilst 'gulfed in full spring-tides
Are lost the murmuring rills.

Ring out ye woodland notes!
Trill through the brightening blue;
Loud swell the anthem new,
Which nature heavenward floats.

For zephyr fannèd river,
For gently swaying trees,
Voice, in each passing breeze,
The praise of life's Great Giver.

Now firelight's lurid gleam
Gives place to greening slope;
Where youth, miraged of hope,
Sees roseate vistas beam.

Hails in each star of eve,
Each lustrous, lengthening day
Of joyous roundelay,
A world where none may grieve.

Blessed morning of the year!
Lone sickness greets the voice
Which waketh to rejoice,
From high to lowliest sphere.

The tiller of the soil
Goes forth in purpose strong;
For Spring's exultant song

Wreathes round the head of toil.

Earth! nurture well the seed;
Sun! gild the swelling grain;
Heaven! sap the thirsty plain;
Till plenty answers need.

Breathe out, Oh genial Spring!
Thy teachings over all;
Till, manna-like, shall fall,
Soft peace where tumults ring.

Then shall the wondrous story
On nature's vivid page
Gleam, till millennial age
Doth flood the world with glory.

# SUMMER.

Hail Summer! glad Summer! thou Queen of the year!
Hail fragrance and beauty encircling thy sphere!
With song of the oriole, with hum of the bee,
We welcome thy coming from far Southern sea.

Thou tintest the blossom on Winter's cold grave;
Bidd'st Commerce ride forth on the white-crested wave;
Thy sweet zephyrs float from the golden-hued west
As whisper of angels from realm of the blest.

The tiniest leaflets which brighten the ground
No less than great waters thy praises resound;
As, peeping from wayside, or climbing the bower,
They kiss the gay sunlight, or drink in the shower.

Heaven's choristers warble in gladsome reply,
As trees offer incense unto thy blue sky;
Even rough ocean, melting to low, passive strain,
Joins earth in harmonious and joyous refrain.

Ah me! for the roses of summer all strewn!
Ah me! for the lives whose brief sunshine has flown!
The clouds often darken at noontide the wave;
The willows oft weep o'er a midsummer's grave.

Oh! for that bright land where no shadows e'er fall;
Nor sickness e'er withers, nor sorrows appall;
Where summers of gladness unceasingly roll
O'er the sinless home of the sanctified soul.

## AUTUMN.

ROBED in thy raiment of splendor,
Thy trappings of purple and gold;
Brighter than vision of dreamland,
Thou lightenest mountain and wold.
Streameth thy rays o'er the woodland;
And the green of the sombre pine,
And the crimson of the maple leaf
Are wreathed in a lustre divine.

Clothed is fair earth of thy fulness;
Enriched is the bloom of the flower;
From verdant to radiant beauty
Thou shadest the gay trellised bower.
Thy smile doth paint the yellow corn;
Thou sing'st in rustle of the sheaves;
Thy symphonies of praise ascend
In twitter of the orchard leaves.

Calm, mellow skies look kindly down
On tree-clad hill, on fruitful vale;
Whilst mariners, on far-off seas,
Hoist canvas to the homeward gale.
Thy generous hand doth fill the cup
With choice reward for labor's crown;
Thy teeming fields revoice that hope
Which blancheth not 'neath Winter's frown.

For though earth's life-sustaining store
Be gathered from her bounteous breast;
Though leafage falls on bare, brown floor,
Though nature lieth long at rest,
The snows shall flit at Spring's warm breath,
And, after Summer's round of cheer,
Again shall Autumn lays peal forth;
Again shall mercy crown the year.

## WINTER.

Down came the rude winds of the Northland;
Their icy breath crusting the snow,
Chilling the mirth of the babbling stream,
Till it sullenly gurgles below.
Freezing the shroud on the lifeless hill,
Erst-while all aglow in its green;
Mocking the gloom of a low-arched sky
By pearl-flashing forest between.

Bitterly keen was that rude, north wind;
I sighed with the outgoing year,
And yearned for the kindlier, warmer suns
Which had waned over Autumn's bier.
That love which haloed the loved of youth,
Which kept unscathed its primal hold,
Outshone the weal of the passing hour;
And harped on nature's minor chord.

As tenderly, up the aisles of time,
Through many a winter's snow
There trilled the long-missed harmonies;
Dear hearts of the long ago!
But—Hush ye voices of plaint within!
Give ear to the voices without;
Over the snow-piles, down the dull street
There pealeth a boy's merry shout.

A tide of youth, with its pleasure freight,
In sunshine of gladness sweeps past;
And clear on the frosty air rings out
"Jolly old Winter's come at last."
Then wholesome trust in the Ever-Good
Welled up over carping unrest;—
I chime in the chime of the changing years;
*They* bow to their Ruler's behest.

# EASTER.

"Fear not!" said the white-robed angel
Who rolled the stone away;
"Fear not, for your Lord is risen;
Come see where Jesus lay."
Oh! joy for the blessed assurance!
No sealed, or guarded grave,
Could bind in its rocky shroudings
The Christ who came to save.

Adown through the circling ages,
As threads of living gold,
The tidings of that hallowed morn
Have spanned life's dreary world.
Have touched, convinced, subdued the soul;
Till reason's twilight ray,
Till vice, and dolesome ignorance
Give place to perfect day.

That voice which awed the angry wave
On deep, blue Galilee,
Yet calms, and rules with mild control,
From nigh to further sea.
Yet wakes to life the desert land,
Breaks superstition's hold;
And, wanderers on the myriad paths,
Doth compass in one fold.

Ye seraphs! strike your golden harps,
Tuned with devotion high;
With echoing pæans sweetly thrill
The arches of the sky.
Whilst we, in noblest measures
Which earthly voices sing,
Yield homage to our risen Lord
Our glorious Saviour—King.

# THANKSGIVING.

In Tisri's holier season,
From City of the Palms
To where onycha incense soared
Amid Hosanna psalms,
Waved green from every housetop,
Gay plumes of laurel tree;
Whilst silver trumpets pealed afar
The tones of victory.
Since through atoning sacrifice
Had dawned the spirit's peace;
And through earth's toil a rich reward
Was reaped, in earth's increase.

Though ruin marks where Tadmor reigned,
And Israel roameth far;
No shoals may stem the mercy-tide;
No power Heaven's largess bar.
Then through the great Atonement's dawn,
Be lit our sin-dimmed eyes;
Till grateful accents pierce the mist,
Into rejoicing skies.
Till garnered fruit, and aftermath;
Till Autumn's tender shine
With farewell tones of woodland song,
Reflect the Love Divine.

# CHRISTMAS EVE.

## I.

Deep shadows mar the pearly snow;
Light flickers on the wall;
While childhood's laugh, as music's flow
Resoundeth through the hall.

Now echoes from the years return;—
Ring out thou pealing bell!
While thought doth last, or memory burn
Thou may'st not strike their knell.

And visions from the earlier days
Within the mind arise,
Illumined by a golden haze;
For earth seems near the skies.

And round our hearth the voices throng
Which tender memories bring;
Those tones which died in even-song,
Those stilled in budding spring.

Once more we gather, as in one,
To list the tale oft told;
That legacy from sire to son
Which waxeth never old.

## II.

No shrill-toned clarion wakes the night
O'er Juda's slumbering plains;
No trumpet blast of armèd might
Sounds forth "Messiah reigns."

No curious crowd demands a sight;
No trophy flameth high;
But seraph hosts, on wings of light,
Haste through the ebon sky.

With glad acclaim His name they sing
Whose praise all heaven doth fill;
At whose command to earth they bring

The message of goodwill.

Oh wonderful! the angels' Lord
In human guise arrayed;
He, by archangels great adored,
Within a manger laid.

Where sages, guided by the star,
Kneel by that Holy One;
As, with rich offerings from afar,
They greet the Virgin's son.

### III.

All lustred with its halo bright
That picture still appears;
Unfading in its glorious light,
Unscathed by lapse of years.

Oh Day of days! we welcome thee;
Bright beam on history's page!
Thou font of youthful hope and glee;
Halt in our pilgrimage.

Those wreaths of red, and green and white,
Which round our altars cling,
Denote, where faith is moved by sight,
His offering, Whom we sing.

The red, the atoning sacrifice;
The white, our souls made clean;
Whilst life unending in the skies
Is typed by evergreen.

Blest beacon o'er our path below!
Thy story, may't extend;
Till in thy pure and perfect glow,
A heaven and earth shall blend.

# CHRISTMAS.

Oh! fair and buoyant Christmas!
Well-spring of childish glee;
Gay jubilance and noisy mirth
Thrill round thy fairy tree.

Oh! roseate flush of Christmas!
Bright vistas crown the day,
When young hearts wake to tenderness
Beneath thy genial ray.

Oh! cheerful, hopeful Christmas!
Rest in the toilsome year;
Thy glory-glimpse illumes the soul;
Earth's cloudlets disappear.

Oh! sweet and tranquil Christmas!
Hours past, and hours to come;
Calm retrospect of vanished joys;
Dear prospect of our home.

Oh! high and holy Christmas!
Unfraught of earthly leaven;
Our spirits chime in angel song,
And near the nearing heaven.

# THE SIEGE OF QUEBEC.

# THE SIEGE OF QUEBEC.

## I.

## PRELUDE.

THOU peerless Queen of peerless land! in nature's choicest zone,
Thou sitt'st in regal dignity upon thy rocky throne;
The glorious memories of the past thy future glories greet,
And fadeless laurels wreathe thy brow, as ocean laves thy feet.
Fair home of faithful, loyal hearts! shrine of the hero-dead!
Whose valor rested not till hid within its gory bed;
Right royal sitt'st thou on thy heights, with Empire's flag unfurled,
The brightest gem, by sea or plain, of all this newer world.

Thou had'st thy skilful mariners, who crossed an unknown sea;
Thou had'st thy famous warriors, thy far-brought peasantry
Who cleared the tangled forest shades, and in the greenwood wild
Prepared an exile's home to lodge the mother with the child.
And thou had'st saints, those holy ones who feared nor shame nor loss,
Who o'er their altars raised aloft the standard of the Cross;
Who suffered torture's keenest pangs, whose souls were winged on high
From bloody knife and cruel flame—such lives may never die.

Softly, Oh winds of the south-land!
Float over valley and steep;
Bathe with your incense of perfume
The spot where the martyrs sleep.

Tenderly, winds of the ocean!
Rippling the streamlet's bright waves.
Pause in your flight o'er the mountains;
Fan with your freshness their graves.

And thou! Oh breeze off the pine-lands!
Far over the glorious West
Sing forth the grandeur of soul-life
From groves where the holy rest.

Where Indian Donacona ruled, there ruled the wise Champlain;
Then Commerce, social herald, brought religion in its train;
Whilst high above thy loftiest crag and by the stately tree
There floated proudly on the breeze the gorgeous *fleur-de-lis*.
And though no more the vine-clad hills should greet the longing eye,
Nor streamlets of the sunny South in joyous strains flash by;
Though never more the worshippers should kneel in ancient fanes,
Yet France as dear, yet faith as bright, might blossom on those plains.

Change copes with time; ills tracked the years; far worse than Indian knife
Came gross misrule and greed of gain, with envious civil strife;
Grim want, foul rapine filled the land and paved the smoother way
For foreign foe and outward wrong, for inward sore decay.
Then followed war with horrors wild, and who a sword could wield
Was summoned to the deadly fray, whilst women tilled the field;
Yet, with a courage native-born within the France of yore,
Thy sons long held a baffled foe from off Canadian shore.

## II.

## THE BOMBARDMENT.

Red glowed the sun of summer morn athwart the shining deep,
All radiant in its still repose, as child in restful sleep;
And as it higher streaked the heavens, and further gilt the wave,
There dawned a sight that chilled stout hearts within those erstwhile brave—
A sight which called the soldier forth to guard his every post,
Which moved the patriot soul to hope, though hope was well-nigh lost;
Had fallen Ticonderoga, Niagara lost the day,
And now the victor's flag streamed out o'er fair St. Lawrence Bay.

A British squadron, fifty sail, with well-trained soldier band,
Led on by Wolfe of martial fame, of skilled and daring hand,
Had anchored on the Orleans coast to watch, if need be wait
Till golden opportunity should crown the course of fate.
'Twas not mere common *role* of arms, to measure strength for strength,
To storm with shot or fiendish shell, to fight at sabre's length;
'Twas to out-plan the well laid scheme, out-match with matchless skill
The great opposing elements, vast work of zealous will.

So huge the perfect system of well arranged defence,
Small marvel if prompt action waived, subdued of grave suspense;
The city, perched upon her heights, in solemn far retreat.
With thousand willing hearts guardant in fealty at her feet;
Along the river's northern rim, to Montmorency's shore,
Redoubt, earthwork and battery defiant aspect bore;
Whilst at each point of access, for miles and miles around,
Stood youth and age, a patriot guard upon a hallowed ground.

High banks and shallow waters, the warships idle lay;

Discouraged and perplexed the Chief, held thus so far at bay;—
Oh, treacherous shining waters! those frowning crags that lave,
Ye folded in your cold embrace eight hundred of the brave,
The bravest of old England, who, fifty years before
Unfighting met their destiny at threshold of that door
Now barred against the invader; much wonder was it then
Though gravest doubt should dull the mind of England's mightiest men?

Mayhap before their vision loomed those feats of former day
When British fleet, in Phipp's command, besieged that fortress grey;
When messenger with flag of truce, was ushered in blindfold
Before the noble Frontenac, that veteran leal and bold.
No coward blood e'er nursed the life of him, the loyal veined,
Proposals for surrender mean, who scornfully disdained;
"Go, tell your General," he said, proud flashed his wrathful eye,
"That surely by my cannon's mouth, shall be my fit reply."

Oft, over dire extremity, a sudden radiance falls;
Though sealed those portals, bullet-proof those adamantine walls,
Swift, as of lightning's vivid flash, Wolfe's eager eye descried
A site for prowess to effect, though skill and force defied.
Where Mount de Levi sits aloft upon the other shore,
Incessant devastation might bridge the waters o'er;
Might bring to woman's, childhood's ears, sore tidings of dismay,
Might picture scenes would dim the eye, through many a lustrous day.

Loud booms along the glistening wave the din of shot and shell;
The breeze-borne notes resound afar a generous people's knell;
The time-worn soldier stands aghast, religion bends the knee,
And silence sceptres ruined homes, where mirth flowed full and free.
Still, firm within thy battlements, upon thy steadfast throne,
Thou beauteous city of the heights! defeat thou would'st not own;
Abode thy Chieftain by thy side, nor left thy ample shield
At tempter's scheme, or skilled device to war on open field.

Yet courage waned not, yet again were outward posts assailed;
But every effort met rebuff, all stratagem had failed;
Who fell not by the Frenchman's arm to perish in their gore
Were fain to find a sure retreat, from off that hostile shore.
Sick of chagrin a fever laid the English leader low,
Ambition, high resolve retired before a stubborn foe;
Were't not that Townshend's able wit one final scheme revealed
Perchance the maple leaf might grace fair Gallia's ancient shield.

## III.

## THE BATTLE.

Out over the quiet waters, in sheen of the starry night,
With sword, and gun, and bayonet, equipped for fervent fight.

On, on by the towering headlands, in shade of frowning steep,
Ere flickering day-dreams banished sweet dreams of friendly sleep.
Ere lingering morn had oped its eyes to greet the orient sun,
They moored beneath a rugged cliff, they scaled it one by one.
Up over moss-hid precipice, with tangled growth o'erhead;—
Well was it he who led the van was of the mountain bred.

Up went the hardy Highlanders, with eye and footing clear,
As when, in their own mountain land, they chased the nimble deer.
O'er broken boughs, through network green, the bright-hued tartan wends
In single file, a living streak with darksome foliage blends.
When, hark! midway the sentry's ear had caught the muffled sound;
He halted the approaching step ere paced his further round.
"*Qui vive?*" he queried; quick response dispelled all fear of wrong;
"*La France,*" came back assuringly; he heard and passed along.

Before the darker hues of night gave place to morning grey,
A force well nigh five thousand strong stood firm in war's array.
They clomb the heights, they chose the ground upon the rearward plain,
Prepared to fight for Britain's might, no worthless prize to gain.
A land of nature's lavish gifts, a store of boundless wealth;
Rare land! where pestilence ne'er stills the bounding pulse of health.
Where, over richly-yielding plains majestic rivers roll;
Where tyranny may forge no chains to bind the freeborn soul.

Though Britain's war-blast sounded forth its warning loud and shrill,
Though Britain's daring rank and file be-crowned the rock bound hill,
Montcalm, undaunted of surprise, with soul to honor dear,
Ne'er faltered in his manly voice, ne'er blanched with heart of fear.
With prompt and steadiest action he ranged his battle plan,
Inspiring with his ardent will the will of lesser man.
Clear ran along the listening lines the order to "Advance,"
And golden eagles waved aloft, and shouts went up for France.

Alas for prudent reckoning! sole valor led the way,
And hasted on to conflict dire, whose only succor lay
In calm, reluctant rallying within their fortress walls,
Till compassed of invading tide, till neared the bugle calls.
Unbroken columns moved ahead; with firm, free step they trod
The plain where many a hero's blood would early damp the sod.
Upon their well matched foe they oped with rain of deadly fire;
The British stirred not from their post, but hailed their presence nigher.

Ho! courage of the mariner who dares the fiercest storm!
Ho! valor of the warrior who fears no hostile form!
Yet braver he who stands erect nor bows the craven head,
Though murderous fire is laying low the living with the dead.
Not theirs to flinch, though comrades fell, theirs only to obey;
Their brave young General had said, and who might say him nay,

As manfully, in face of death, he hasted to and fro;
"Reserve your fire till forty yards divide you from the foe."

See Europe's proudest martial powers with rival flag unfurled;
Intent in blood to seal the fate of this fair Western world.
To plant upon those echoing heights that standard which would gleam
O'er sea-wide lakes, o'er prairie vast, o'er forest, mount and stream.
The ancient feuds, the after-curse of many a needless fray,
The jealousies of race and creed revive their wonted sway,
Impart a zest to willing minds, a force to vigorous hand,
And nerve the soldier's arm to fight for king and fatherland.

On came brave Gallia's war-like sons; shone helm, and sword, and plume;
On like a mountain cataract which rushes to its doom
Of loss amid the foaming surge that sweeps o'er ocean bed;
So more the surge of battle sweep o'er many a noble head.
No further halt! the voice is raised, the expectant order given,
When, loud as if a thunder bolt had rent the vaulted heaven,
Out belched from thousand iron throats a thousand tongues of fire;
Out flashed the British musketry as torch for funeral pyre.

The blow long pending, did its work among the assailing host;
Who stood the shock, through blinding smoke could see that all was lost.
Still Montcalm strove, with voice of cheer, due order to retain;
His veterans, by a small redoubt, he marshalled once again.
But vain! ah vain, his arduous task! the stronghold of Quebec
Was doomed to slip from Gallia's hand;—yet rise from out the wreck
A queenly city on the wave, a beacon on the sea,
Fair monument of Britain's might in Canada the free!

Short space the balance wavered—one fierce and final blow,
And the flower of Europe's chivalry on foreign field lay low.
Ere golden beams of noontide spread their glory o'er the sky,
The plain was sodden, far and near, with streams of crimson dye,
And din of battle slackened, save tread of flying feet—
Pursuers hurrying onward to intercept retreat;
Whilst on the field of carnage, of groans and shattered spear,
The rival Chieftains won their right to grace red glory's bier.

Serene of soul in youth's bright dawn, Wolfe laid him down to die;
From strife profound, from mortal pain, peace gently closed his eye.
Whilst Montcalm, loyal to the core, avowed with parting breath
His greatest guerdon in defeat, to die a soldier's death.
True brotherhood of heroism! in God's eternal laws,
One equal spirit ruled their course, however adverse their cause.
And high on pedestal of Fame, where victors bear the palm,
Beside the British General there stands the brave Montcalm.

## IV.

## THE SURRENDER.

Just Spirit! from the empyrean heights, regard this lower clime!
From anthems of eternity, from angel theme sublime
Look down upon those woe-worn lives, replete of misery!
Stretch forth Thine arm to stem the tide of mortal agony!
The groaning years have waited long to hail the reign of peace,
Omnipotence give forth Thy word, bid war and tumult cease!
Then harmony shall tune its chords; for plaintive, low-voiced song
Rejoicings of a ransomed world shall seraph notes prolong.

Since passion waged the bloody deed that slew by Eden's gate,
The earth hath borne its bitter fruit of envy's cruel hate;
Even God in man is crushed beneath insatiate thirst of gain,
A thirst unquenched though streams of blood have purpled earth and main.
Oh rarely beauteous, blooming world! why should the true and brave,
Whilst meaner souls usurp thy joys, claim but in thee a grave!
Thou, Oh Supreme! Whose glory lit confusion's dreary night,
Out cast the chaos of the years, inflood Thy glorious light!

Power Benign! Thy influence shed, the brutal passions tame!
Let pure and holy altar light, from clear cerulean flame,
Beam into dark and vile recess of evil's inmost heart!
Incite the nobler sentiments to act the nobler part!
Then war no more shall devastate the work of toilsome hand,
Nor wailing tones of hunger-pain sigh o'er a fruitful land;
Into Oblivion's direst shades shall wrong and woe be hurled,
And cycles of millennial bliss illume a sinless world.

Dragged up were the ponderous guns, dragged up the slippery hill;—
What task too hard for British hands when backed by British will?
Impelled o'er war-worn field of death, of visage stained and scarred,
Till set against the citadel, a grim, relentless guard.
Out echoes through the silent streets the cannon's dolesome boom,
The famine-struck are fain to feel sure bodings of their doom;—
Four lingering days of torture, when exhausted nature calls
To sheathe the patriot sword and leave the long-loved native halls.

Full tenderly the mellow light of Autumn's tranquil hours
In splendor decked the forest shades and gilt the wayside flowers,
Rose-tinted all the fleecy clouds which flecked the arc of blue,
Reflecting on the sullen wave a brighter, warmer hue.
Yet, in its placid majesty, from out that sky serene,
That Autumn sun looked down upon a sad and bitter scene;
Starvation's wan and wasted cheek, the crushed soul of the brave,
The tomb of those who nobly earned a patriot-soldier's grave.

Lay down thine arms, Oh, hero-heart! thou shamest not thy crest;
They own no coward vassalage who bow at Heaven's behest;
Though from the river and the tree there vanisheth for aye
The ensign which so proudly bore the brunt of many a fray,
Yet honor bideth with thee still, and though thy *fleur-de-lis*
Is grafted in the English rose, thou bend'st a faithful knee
At thy faith's shrine; thy language lives, nor shall thy glory fade
While snows o'ermantle mountain steep, or zephyrs fan the glade.

Thou, Conqueror! whose ancient flag floats out on every breeze,
Whose power is felt, whose might is owned by nigh and further seas;
To thee is given a wider scope within this sphere of change,
To work out mightier designs upon a vaster range,
Thwart not thy royal prestige, hold not thy royal hand,
But open wider, still more wide, this haven for every land;
This boundless, fair, Canadian land—land of especial grace,
Where freedom yieldeth equal rights to every creed and race.

Still, peerless Queen of peerless land! in nature's choicest zone
Thou sitt'st in regal dignity upon thy rocky throne;
The glorious memories of the past thy future glories greet,
And fadeless laurels wreathe thy brow, as ocean laves thy feet.
Fair home of faithful, loyal hearts! shrine of the mighty dead!
Whose valor rested not till hid within its gory bed;
Right royal sitt'st thou on thy heights, with Empire's flag unfurled,
The brightest gem by sea or plain of all this Western World.

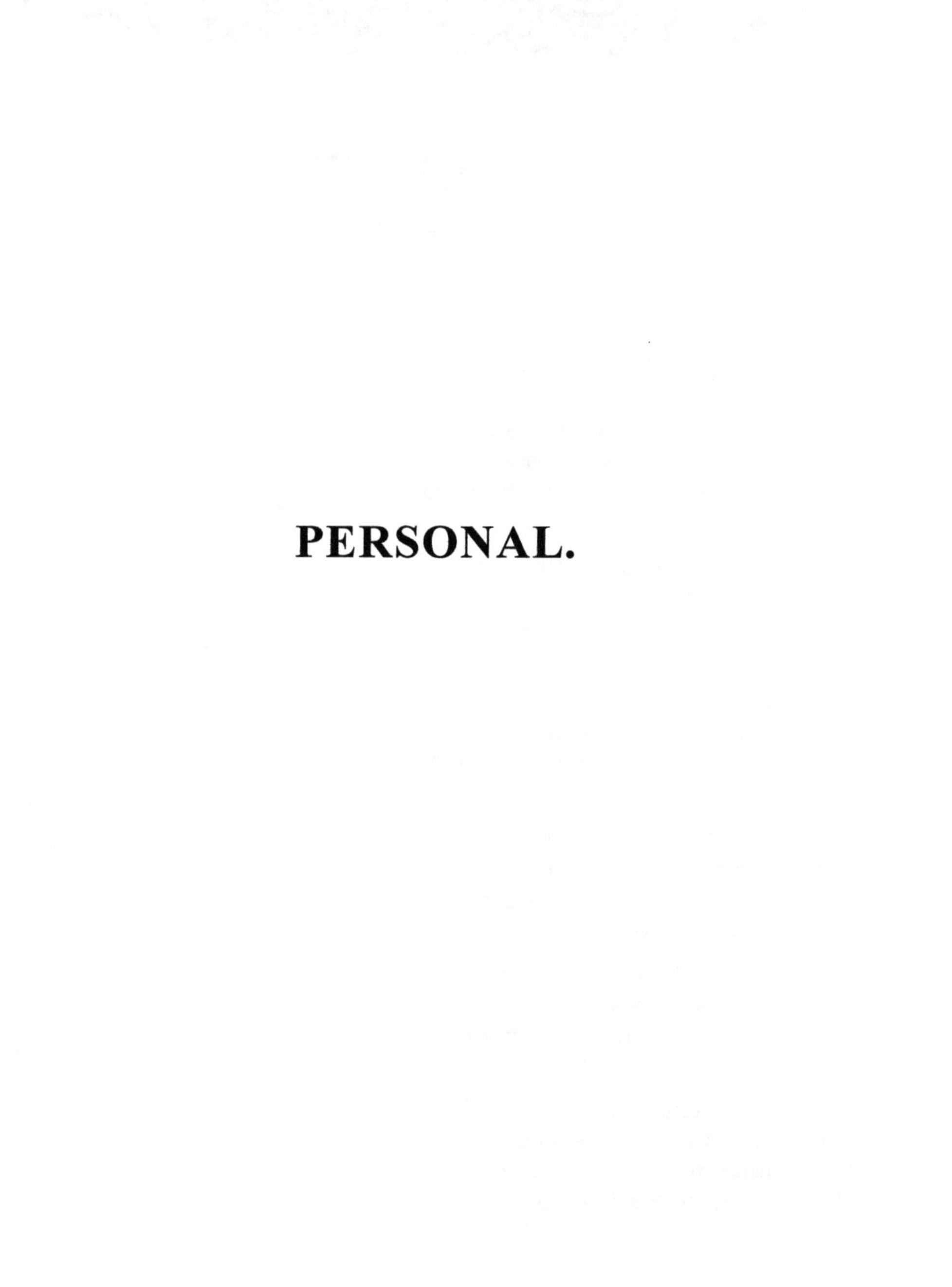

# PERSONAL.

# OUR QUEEN.

### MAY 24TH.

LOVED Queen of Scotia's bonnie braes!
Of Erin's, England's homes;
This day thy people speak thy praise
Where'er the exile roams.

By gorgeous India's ancient fanes;
On Greenland's banks of snow;
Where, o'er Columbia's boundless plains,
Majestic rivers flow.

On frozen seas, in balmy air,
By forest's dusky green
Ariseth up to heaven the prayer:—
"God bless our gracious Queen!"

God guide her through the evening light
To where no shadows frown;
Nor sorrow's pall, nor darksome night
Will dim *that* lustrous crown.

Let earthly glory sink in night;
Life's record, without stain,
Shall cast an ever-hallowed light
Across Victoria's reign.

'Tis not that Britain's martial prow
In every port appears;
Nor that the flag which streameth now
Hath waved a thousand years.

'Tis not the sceptre, nor the sword,
Nor gold, nor precious stone;
True sympathy hath knit the cord
That binds us to the Throne.

Thy sires, in siege and battle field
Full bravely bore their part;
But, without strife to thee doth yield
The fortress of the heart.

Not land from weakling nations rent
Shall keep thy memory green;
But this—thy lasting monument—
She was *the peoples' Queen*.

# THE PRINCESS OF WALES

**1863—1892.**

SEEMS it yestreen since we
First hailed thee, beautous bride!
Sweet-smiling, by the side
Of Him, our king to be.

Cheek of the pink sea-shell;
Eyes of the summer blue,
Locks of the brown-gold hue;
Voice clear as silver bell.

The myriads crowd the street;
Glad music, nigh and far,
Outsoundeth earthly jar;
And tenders welcome meet.

* * * * *

Once more thy form I see,
Amid thy family band
Save one, on Scottish strand,
And twain—where seraphs be.

Nor fled thy winsome grace;
Nor did thy beauty fade,
Though sad bereavement's shade
Hath paled thy peerless face.

Still sway with gentle hand;
Still live thy lovesome life
Fond mother! faithful wife!
First princess of first land.

# CANADA
# TO
# H. R. H. PRINCE GEORGE.

**MAY 4TH, 1893.**

TIME was when tyrants reigned,
When law was law for naught;
When man, with mind distraught,
Knelt with allegiance feigned.

Now, in these ampler days
When dews of peace distil,
When all may climb who will,
Just souls may justly praise.

Ours was thine earlier sorrow;
Ours is thy later joy;
No base, unmeet alloy;
No faithless, vague to-morrow.

But tender, soulful, true;
O'er leagues of greening plain,
From east to western main,
'Neath all our brightening blue.

Knit by love's kindred tie,
Heart wafteth unto heart
Weal, time nor space may part:
Best gift from low or high.

Best gifts, Oh Prince! be thine
In whom our hopes repose;
Thine, and thy English Rose;
Till crowned of crown divine.

# GLADSTONE.

VAIN be the rare genius of sage or of scholar,
Philosophy's nursling, or gifted of song;
Vain, minds of rich culture, with tones of choice music,
If cradled in falsity, nurtured in wrong.

But cloudless the intellect sunned of fair Freedom;
Full lofty the soul which, with feelings refined,
Doth lift up a voice for the weal of the nations;
Ennobling with sympathy all of his kind.

Fair Freedom! thou star in the night of the ages!
Thou radiant in fervor! thou essence divine!
He! highest in soul-height, doth build up thine altars;
While devotees faithful, bend low at thy shrine.

The far-seeing wisdom of mercy which hailed thee,
Hath wooed thee to listen the suppliant's song;
Hath wooed and hath won thee through love, lit of reason;—
Heaven's benison laurel the healer of wrong!

# SIR JOHN A. MACDONALD.

**BORN 11TH JAN., 1815—DIED 6TH JUNE, 1891.**

DIMMED thy bright eyes, Oh Canada!
Bedimmed with the incense of woe;
Hushed thy young joy-peals of laughter;
Whose heart beat to thine lieth low.
Great heart! which, in truest devotion,
Kept faith to its earliest shrine;
Great land! widely girthed of each ocean;
His lifetime of service was thine.

Well mays't thou weep, yet not repine;
Rude wert thou, an untutored child,
When first his strong, firm hand clasped thine,
And led thee o'er thy boundless wild,
And cleared the mists from thy young eyes,
As with magician's gifted wand;
Till Hope's bright dawn illumed thy skies,
And glorified this boundless land.

The mind astute discerned thy force;
The springs of plenty watered dearth;
Then rose, from infound, ample source,
The mightiest structure on this earth:
The home where freeborn souls are free;
Where, 'neath blue skies, o'er rich green sod
No worship bends the humble knee,
Save homage to fair Freedom's God.

Though sore thy heart, Oh Canada!
Grudge not thy Chief his well-earned rest;
The veteran who hath braved the strife
May fold his arms o'er peaceful breast.
Droop banners o'er his honored bier!
Strew *immortelles* of every clime!
His larger life, in nobler sphere,
Is bounded not with hedge of time.

## HON. ALEX. MACKENZIE.

### BORN 28TH JANY., 1822—DIED 17TH APRIL, 1892.

DRAW nigh with reverence, Canada!
Beyond all strain of mortal toil
He lieth, with unstainèd crest
Calm-sleeping on his chosen soil.
No higher boon may patriot crave
Than grateful country's honest tear;
Whilst Faith, outreaching 'yond the grave,
With stainless emblem decks the bier.

Rare mind! firm as the granite stone
From out thy much-loved Scottish hills;
Soul! clear as sunlight's upper zone
When smiling o'er Canadian rills.
Oh! well for thee, belovèd land!
That, ripening to thy golden prime,
Stout hearts, and faithful held thine hand
And led thee on to ampler time.

Embalm his memory, Canada!
Nor taint with ill his honored name
Who loved thee dearer than his life;
Who, serving thee, rejected fame.
Not now, through many an after year;
In cool, calm retrospect of time,
Shall all his sterling worth appear,
In grandeur fitting and sublime.

Though stilled the aims of lofty end;
Though leaders in the field lie low;
Heaven's purposes shall onward tend,
As ocean wavelets shoreward flow.
Wail not! *he* walketh in the light
His work, imbued with high intent,
Doth magnify a country's might,
And build his fairest monument.

# IN MEMORIAM.[4]

Falling! all noiselessly falling!
Dim-golden, and russet and grey;
Leaves of the Autumn soul telling,
Earth's loveliness passeth away.

*Here* the rich strains of rare music,
Borne upwards of summer's soft gale,
Are lost in the sigh of earth's sorrows,
Or sunk in bereavement's sad wail.

*There* shall dear households long severed
Rejoice in the anthem sublime;
Hosannas of spirits united
Shall echo o'er dirges of time.

Sickness and pain shall evanish;
The years, with their sorrow shall cease;—
O'er the glad souls of the ransomed
Eternity rolleth in peace.

---

[4] "In Memoriam."—In memory of the pious and charitable Mrs. M. M. T. Hodgson, daughter of the late Hon. J. Brecken, and wife of the Hon. Edward J. Hodgson, Master of the Rolls of P. E. Island, Canada; who died on the 19th October, 1889.

## BISHOP MACINTYRE.

ON Canaan's border land,
By Jordan's watery gates,
The host of Israel waits;—
They mourn the Guiding-Hand.

With firm, free step he trod
On Pisgah's mountain crest;
He laid him down to rest;
Alone! save with his God.

He sighed no faint farewell;
No murmuring refrains
Out-echoed angel strains;
Nor tolled dull funeral knell.

Thus, as in days gone by
Great leader! careful guide!
God called thee hence, aside;
We might not see thee die.

Yet we have seen—may see
Thy work of nobler life;
The courage through the strife;
Deeds testify of thee.

Rest well! Oh silvered head!
Voice ever prone to bless,
To soothe the soul's distress,
Peace to thy lowly bed!

Though next thy heart, thine own;
Thy sympathies, world wide
Flowed, with unstinted tide;
Bedewed each mortal zone.

Rest well! ye feet which trod
That straight and narrow way
Illumed of purer ray;
Quintessence of our God.

Soul! which hath soared afar,
Beyond the flight of time;
In calm, congenial clime,

No ills thy joys may mar.

Fair spirit! just and wise;
Kind heart of largess love!
Christ-life, all creeds above;
Rest thou in kindred skies.

More glorious eve's bright sun,
More dull seems dolesome night;
So, lost thy glorious light;
And yet—Heaven's will be done.

# BISHOP BROOKS.

## THE STUDENTS OF HARVARD AWAITING THE FUNERAL CORTEGE.

Why, with uncovered head
Stand they upon that fleece of snow
Mute-stricken, as of sudden woe?
Silent they wait the dead.

Comes there some hero slain
Upon the blood-red field of war?
With soldier-guarded funeral car,
And glittering martial train.

No gun with sullen roar;
No flaunting emblems from the fight
To spread his fame, to tell his might;
Who died, to die no more.

With reverend tread, and slow,
All noiselessly the footsteps fall;
As sombre garb, and plume and pall
Pass o'er the soft, white snow.

'Mid Love's choice offering
Of sweet, rare flowers, whose tender breath
Speak brightest life, serenest death,
He lies, affection's king.

Triumph of Christian faith
O'er spurious sophistries of time;
The sinless walk; the end sublime,
No ghastly fears to scathe.

Pass on unto thy rest
Thou generous heart! thou rich in lore!
Thou whom all creeds and castes deplore;—
God knoweth what is best.

# AFTER MANY YEARS.

If e'er from holier heights there sped
One attribute divine,
To rest upon a mortal head,—
That head, dear love! was thine.

True worth beyond expression towers;
Excess in language mars;—
What artist e'er inspired the flowers,
Or lighted up the stars?

# TENNYSON.

## ANSWER TO "CROSSING THE BAR."

CLEAR-SHINING, evening star!
We make no moan for thee
Who sightest, 'yond the bar,
Blest immortality!

Yet, at thy farewell tone,
Thou glorious poet-king!
The tears unbidden spring
From peoples of each zone.

So long, from loftier sphere,
Thy pure and lustrous rays
Have lit earth's sombre ways:—
No sky may own thy peer.

Oh, never-dying song!
Oh, princely legacy!
Till life shall living be
Thou'lt thrill, the years along.

Mist wreathe, or ocean foam;
The beacon shineth clear,
The joy-bells sound anear,
Beyond the bar is—Home!

Clear-shining, evening star!
We make no moan for thee
Who sightest 'yond the bar,
Blest immortality.

# SPURGEON.

### "NOTHING BUT FAITH."

THINE was no faith of pulseless form,
Of actor, acting well his *role*;
Or deeming, through mere solemn rites,
To nourish the immortal soul,
Nor thine that bare and stunted growth,
To limits of a sect confined;
Expanding not in broader realm
Than atmosphere by man defined.

Nor thine that crude philosophy
Whose meteor-flash hath oft beguiled
The traveller from clear mountain heights,
To perish on the misty wild.
No gloomy cypress wreath for thee!
Oh brow unkenned of bigot frown!
Fair coronet of laurel leaves;
Meet emblem of thy fadeless crown.

Bright as the pure, cerulean arch,
*Thy* faith all creeds and rites doth span
And sees, through Love's refining lens,
The Deity in brother man.
With active, humanizing power,
Uplifts the soul, low sunk in sin;
Till, yielding to its tender touch,
The chains unbar—God enters in.

# BEECHER.

## THE LAST TIME IN PLYMOUTH CHURCH.

THE organ grandly pealed;
Still rose the peaceful hymn;
The lights, though waxing dim,
A beauteous sight revealed.

From off the busy street
Into the sacred pile,
Adown the shadowy aisle
Came little wandering feet.

Secure from fear of harm,
With eager, upturned face,
The lone ones rest a space;
Joy-filled of music's charm.

Forgot their hapless fate;
Forgot cold, worldling scorn;
Unseen the life forlorn;
Seems nigh heaven's golden gate.

Upriseth from his seat
He of a world-wide fame;
He of the lustrous name,
Those nameless ones to greet.

The mightiest orb on high
Doth kiss the meanest flower;
True love, in bounteous shower,
Doth rift earth's formal sky.

Stoops low the silvered head
To kiss the smooth young brow,
To seal the sacred vow
Which life-long fragrance shed.

And tenderly his arms
Those boyish forms enfold;
As if, o'er life's drear wold,
He'd shield from rude alarms.

Thus pass they from the sight,
From out the vaulted door;—
*He* walks the pearly floor,
*They* grope through dismal night.

Oh scene surpassing fair!
Soul-filling, all sublime;
Undimmed of dark'ning time,
Unlit of earthly glare.

Fair soul of tenderness!
Unselfish, meek and mild,
The waif, the outcast child
Thou deignest to caress.

Sweet, humanizing love!
Beyond choice gifts of mind,
'Yond culture most refined;
Bright essence from above!

Columbia! brave young land!
Long is thy scroll of fame;
Full many a deathless name
Hath led thee by the hand.

High on that scroll of fame,
Whilst hero echoes ring,
Whilst votaries pause to sing,
Shall glow thy Beecher's name.

# ALLELUIA.

No more upon Parnassus' hill
Thou'lt string thy patriot lyre;
To tell those feats which nations thrill,
Which youthful spirits fire.
How, on the blood-red battle field
Great heroes fall, but never yield;
True courage is the only shield
Thy whole-souled Briton owns.

No more thou'lt sing thy graceful lays
Of rock, and mount, and stream;
Or cause the light from Heaven's pure rays
O'er nature's face to beam.
We heard the rustle of the tree,
The humming of the busy bee,
When nature waked to life with thee
In joyous harmony.

But though thy harp is silent now,
And hearts may mourn thee long;
Where halos crown the victor's brow
Thou sing'st the angels' song.
Dust mingles with its kindred dust,
Soul joins the army of the just;—
Their Leader was thy hope and trust
Through life's long pilgrimage.

## “THREE YEARS.”

HERE the pain, and gloom and sorrow,
Here the household lone and sad;
*There* the ever-bright to-morrow,
There the youthful spirit glad.
*Here* the parents vigil keeping
O'er the beauteous head laid low;
*There* the eyes which know no weeping
Shall with rapture ever glow.

Bright as were the sunny tresses
Curling o'er the fair, young brow,
Richer far the crown that presses
Round his seraph forehead now.
Clear and chaste as crystal seemeth,
Worthless is it 'side the gem;
So, howe'er earth's beauty gleameth,
Pales its 'fore Heaven's diadem.

Now, his gracious word believing,
Who on earth with woe did weep,
Mingle trustful joy with grieving
O'er the loved, who rests in sleep.
For, where groups of children gather,
He hath joined the choir of praise
Which, around our Heavenly Father,
Chants the hymn of deathless days.

## THE EVENING STAR.

I sit me down at eventide
Day's cares receding far,
When sweet! a whisper at my side,
"Mama, come see my star!"

"The only one in all the sky
Away up—Oh, so far!
And yet it shines so beautiful,
My own, dear, lovely star!"

Oh! child of many hopes and fears;
Of many an anxious thought;
Oh life! with parents' prayers and tears,
So oft from Heaven besought.

If spared to pass the tender years
Of infancy and truth;
God keep thee through the slippery path
Of boyhood, and of youth.

And guide thee by His own right hand
In wisdom's pleasant way;
And never in foul vice's snares
Permit thy feet to stray.

And when that love which gazeth now
Into thy sunny eyes
Can only come, at God's good will
In message from the skies.

Oh! should the tempter's net be spread,
Look upward! do not fear;
From 'yond thy star, a mother's love
Will shine thy way to cheer.

If e'er thou reachest manhood's prime,
'Mid pleasures of this world
Let ever, in truth's sacred cause
Thy banner be unfurled.

May all the graces which adorn
Great minds in thee excel;
May't long be said of thee "he served

His generation well."

Thy emblem be yon evening star;
Aye steady in its light;
Calm-peering o'er a world of change;
Ne'er stooping from its height.

When darkness deepens all around,
And rivals fill the field;
Let faith and courage arm thy soul,
And form thy radiant shield.

Then, when thy golden hue of morn
Gives place to sober grey;
And years which never-ending seem
Have fled like one short day.

Relying on that Mighty One
Who raised the starry frame;
Who through life's changes, toils and tears,
Abideth still the same.

Thy feet shall out the swelling flood,
Step safe upon the strand;
And mayhap then, a mother's love
Again shall clasp thy hand,
And lead thee, 'yond thy shining star,
Into the deathless land.

# RHYMES OF ANCIENT ROME.

# HORATIUS. B.C. 650.

**B.C. 650.**

A PLAN of fair devising when battle feuds were rife;
To save by lesser sacrifice, a needless waste of life.
Three brothers Curiatii, choice of the Alban band,
Against three brothers Horatii, Rome's proffered champions, stand;
Should Horatii assert their might, the Alban arms would yield,
If Curiatii, then should Rome to servile fate be sealed.

Well fought those manly combatants in sight of either host;
The struggle wavered long and keen, high hopes were rudely tossed;
But strength, upborne of courage, wanes before time's fatal throes,
The brave may strive yet striving fall, as fell those rival foes
Save one, who owed to strategy what prowess might not yield,
A Horatii stood conqueror on Alba's blood-stained field.

Rome is avowed the victor, the battle-sword is sheathed,
And round Horatius' youthful head gay triumph's crown is wreathed:
'Mid gratulations of the camp, 'mid cheerings of the throng
The hero who hath slain to save, is proudly borne along,
When Hark! beyond the joyous notes which stir the balmy air
Upwafteth to his ears the sad reproaches of despair.

"Oh! woe for my belovèd!
My love who loved me so;
Oh cruel hand! Oh evil fate!
Which laid the mighty low.

"Oh brother! dearly hast thou earned
Thy country's noblest boon;
Thou'st quenched the lustre of my life
Ere reached its bright, high noon.

"Thou comest laden rich with spoils,
Thy valor to attest;
One only trophy greets mine eye,
*His* cloak upon thy breast.

"Go! list the plaudits of the crowd
Whose liberties you save;
One only voice thrills through my soul,
*That* voice from out the grave.

"For thee shall golden goblets pour,
And glorious rosebays twine;
For me—my heart lies low with his
Whose heart was wholly mine."

Oh maiden! for that prudence which looks beyond the hour;
Oh for that subtle wisdom which holds the key of power!
For calm and callous reasoning, which worketh out its plan,
Which checketh honest principle, and dupeth craft of man.
As in these nigher ages, so in those earlier days,
Keen wit, cool wisdom e'er dissolve beneath Love's fervent rays.

Is it fatigue of battle? why pales the warrior now?
Is it chagrin in triumph's hour which clouds that martial brow?
Both lend their aid, yet greater far than aught on earth beside,
The sore and bitter struggle 'twixt love and wounded pride;
'Twixt patriot-love and brother-love, the love of life's young day;
When sympathy of sisterhood charmed every grief away.

Horatius paused; out flashed the sword which drank her lover's blood;
He plunged it in his sister's heart, he slew her where she stood;
And, as he sheathed the reeking blade which struck the dastard blow,
"So perish every maid" he said "who wails a Roman foe!"
Oh cruel fate! Oh hapless twain! Oh tragic scenes of old!
Go! thank high Heaven these later times are cast in Christian mould.

# PYRRHUS. B.C. 280.

### AFTER HIS DEFEAT OF THE ROMAN ARMY.
### B.C. 280.

"If these were my soldiers," he said,
As he glanced o'er the gory field
Where mingled the dying and dead
Of foemen who knew not to yield.
"If these were my soldiers, with standard unfurled,
I should gather the reins of a vanquished world.

"Seven times did we charge on the foe;
As oft did we order retreat;
Seven times, till the ebb and the flow
Brought the battle-tide under our feet.
Yet, unto destruction their courage held fast,
Till destiny weighted the balance at last.

"A victor! yet mourning the lost!
The flower of my army, my pride,
Who led in the conquering host
Lie mute as the serfs by their side.
Oh! mothers of Epirus, what shall atone!
Must the victor ride back with his laurels—alone!

"Unmatched as to numbers we met;
Well mated in ardor we fought;
Ah! never was victory yet
With bloodier sacrifice bought.
Peace be to our dead 'neath Lucanian sods!
Let Valour high-niche them in shrine of the gods!

"But *these*! of Rome's valiant who fell;
Who flinched not, but met every blow
With prowess no language may tell;
With face ever set to the foe.
If these were *my* soldiers, with standard unfurled,
I should reign, the one king of a whole conquered world."

So is it in life's bitter warfare;
When hosts of wrong-doing assail,
The bravest in spirit, the truest of soul

In heat of the battle oft fail.
They lack in a leader, they parry each blow,
Yet fall in the conflict with face to the foe.

Legions of evil confronting
Firm-footed, position maintain;
Look thou to thine able Commander!
The foeman shall muster in vain.
In phalanx well marshaled, with standard unfurled,
Thou shalt combat and conquer a whole sinning world.

# MARIUS. B.C. 86.

## SEATED ON THE RUINS OF CARTHAGE. B.C. 86.

WHAT voiceth thy bright waters? Oh Sea of the summer clime!
Thou mirror of life's history! thou orator sublime!
What sing thy laughing wavelets as they dance along thy shore?
What moan thy heaving surges, as they sway with sullen roar?
Thou tellest to the breezes soft, which fan thy breast of pride,
That pomp and glory of a world once nestled by thy side;
Thou singest, in the purling wave, quaint rhythms of romance,
Of witching queens and warriors bold, of siege and glistering lance;
Thou wailest, in sad monotone, o'er empires gone for aye;
Thou smilest in benign repose upon this freer day.

Alone on the crumbling ruins! bowed low his agèd head;
Life's wreck 'mid shattered monuments, sole mourners o'er the dead;
Meet emblem of capricious fate, which scorns decrees of man;
Meet site for an exile's musing on Treachery's subtle plan.
Great city of the salt sea wave, on Afric's burnished shore!
That gleaming wave which wailed the dirge of those it proudly bore
To battle in a vain defense, to sleep the sleep profound
Within no sculptured sepulchre, beneath no hallowed ground.
Great Carthage the magnificent! when Slaughter rung thy knell,
Even from thy victor's war-strained eyes, unwonted tear-drops fell.

A fugitive sat Marius; despondent and alone;
Well-nigh forgot of enemies, forsaken of his own.
Where now that voice of terror, those eyes of flashing light
Which awed the Cymbrian jailor, which urged his coward flight?
Where now that haughty form and mien which led the Roman bands
To smite Europa's barbarous hordes back from the classic lands?
Mute are the plaudits of the crowd, seared are the harvest sheaves;
Quenched the chimera light of flame, which gilt the laurel leaves;
Had vanished, as a taunting sprite, those dreams ambition nursed;
The very stones on which he sat were of the gods accursed.

Which is the happier? he who strives the higher heights to gain,
Or he who mingles in the crowd that throngs the nether plain?
Ask ye Ambition's tortured brain if vulgar hue and cry
The craving of the loftier mood doth fully satisfy:

Ask of keen Avarice if its hoard e'er soothed a sin-fraught breast,
Or purchased peace of mind, or charmed a conscience into rest.
I wot 'tis safer far to bide in calm contentment's vale,
And o'er the placid inland seas to peaceful moorings sail.
Even those whose largess, honest worth doth merit just renown
What are they save the shining mark for Envy to uncrown.

Doth muse Oh Marius! on that hour when blasts of martial horn
Across thy peasant heritage through haunts of toil were borne?
When thy young heart throbbed high to join that glittering array,
Which owned thee chief in valor's van through many an after day.
Dost storm Numantia's battlements, whence arrows showered as rain?
Dost stand in thickest of the fight on crimsoned fields of Spain?
Or sittest thou an honored guest, where flows the festive tide?
Thy plebeian birth no barrier, by Africanus' side?
Dost list that certain prophecy that should his race be run,
The mantle of his might should fall on thee, great Valor's son?

Raise up thy head, Oh Marius! look forth ayond the wave!
Yield not to dire despondency; ills conquer not the brave;
Think of thy former exile, then of that glorious hour
When suffrage of the multitude invested thee with power:
When Rome's patricians bent the knee around thy self-built throne,
And all the wills of every land succumbed unto thine own:
Though Envy forged the coward chains which dragged thy scepter down,
It may not wrest from memory thy record of renown;
Arise! reward of courage waits, the dismal night is o'er;
That sun is dawning which will flush thy Civic crown once more.

# BRUTUS. B.C. 42.

### THE LAST CAMPAIGN.
### B.C. 42.

THE warrior doffed his heavy helm,
Unclasped the sheath from off his breast;
He turned aside from sword and lance,
Yet sought no couch of needful rest.

His soul was filled with new, strange dread,
Since haunting ghosts of evil done
Uprose, and banished from his mind
All war plans for the rising sun.

Again the blazing holocaust
Of patriot Xanthus greets his eyes;
Again before his ruthless hand
The plundered Lycian peasant flies.

Once more within the Senate House
He lists those accents, full and clear,
Which plead the sacred rights of Rome;—
Brave warrior! statesman without peer!

He sees the quivering sunbeams play
Upon the sandal's burnished gold;
And light the gorgeous Tyrian dyes
Which deck that form of princely mould,

Then stream o'er proud, patrician crest
Down to the swaying mass below;
Whose wills imbibe the speaker's will,
As well aimed darts from high strung bow.

Ingrate, he joins the dastard few
That round the mighty Cæsar stand,
And stains his weapon to the hilt
With noblest blood in Roman land.

He hears the astonished "Brutus, thou!"
He marks the sad, reproachful eye,
Ere, wrapped within the toga folds,
The lofty head bows down to die.

No war blast wakes a sleeping world;
Deep silence broodeth o'er the camp;
Still, careless as to wanted rest
Sits Brutus by the flickering lamp.

Is it a phantom, that giant form,
Or spirit to human shape lent,
Which glideth, with never a warning,
From shadow land into the tent?

Of stature majestic; erect;
Terrific of feature, stern-eyed;
No token, save only a look;
Such look as all welcome defied.

"Thy name," said the awe struck warrior
"Thy name and thy purpose unfold?"
His tones wore the mask of fortitude,
But the stream from his heart ran cold.

"My name"—and the dark scowl deepened
As the lips of the mystic unsealed;
"My name is—thy genius of evil;—
We shall meet on Philippi's red field!"

Hushed were the dire, prophetic tones;
The vision vanished as it came;
But, from that hour in Brutus' soul
Was crushed Ambition's furious flame.

No more he dreamt to enter Rome
In laurel-wreathed triumphal car;
With captive monarchs in his train,
With spoils and trophies from afar.

Nor e'er to quaff the festive bowl
'Neath purple canopy of state;
Whilst bard and sage his feats rehearse,
And martial throngs his bidding wait.

Ah, Cæsar! thou wert well avenged,
When on its lowly, greenwood bed,
Defeated valour stooped to swell
The army of ignoble dead.

Though on those ancient battle-fields,
Sapped with the blood of myriad slain,
The suns of centuries have smiled,
And reapers gathered golden grain.

Though pomp and power of ancient Rome
With Roman idols passed away,
The thirst of power, and greed of gain

Live on to mar this later day.

Still boastful arrogance excels,
And moneyed ignorance soareth high;
Still fashion rules the world of sham;
Still man for man in strife must die.

Yet, sure as rills from mountain source
Through varied channels seaward run;
So surely ill will track the course
Of him that hath the evil done.

And conscience seared, lethargic-souled,
Who deal in evil to the last
Must realize, beyond the bourne,
Deservèd doom, and mercy past.

# MARCUS CURTIUS.

## A LEGEND.

Still, in these balmier days of Rome,
The mother tells her child
That once, within the Forum, oped
A chasm deep and wild.

That every heart, with horror chilled,
Unto the altar hied;
Soothsayers, augurs sought the cause,
Yet answer was denied.

At length an agèd seer proclaimed,
"The gods will vengeance wreak,
Till choicest gift, cast in the gulf,
Doth penitence bespeak."

The mother shuddering, clasps her babe
More closely to her breast;
The warrior who ne'er feared a foe
Bends low his mailèd crest.

The heartless miser hugs his gold;
Affection claims its own;
Yet, mystery beyond all ken,
Such gifts might ill atone.

'Neath blackened sky the wind moans on,
Wide yawns the dark abyss;—
Oh Heavens! was ever sore suspense
Or terror like to this!

*   *   *   *   *

Hark! sweet as angel symphony,
"'Tis found! the offering's found!"
And forward press the eager throng
To find due vantage ground.

What star descendeth through the gloom
To rift dark sorrow's night?
Is't hero from the battle field,
Or monarch girt with might?

Up rides young Marcus Curtius
Upon his milk white steed;
No word, but waving of the hand,
As he dashes on with speed.

Unto the dreary chasm's mouth;—
The frighted charger springs,
He rears, he snorts, and foamy flakes
O'er Curtius' armor flings.

Fair picture for all spheres and times!
Upon death's borderland,
One gleam of sunshine for his crown,
See Rome's self martyr stand!

He gently soothed his noble horse;
Then, as from silver bell,
Upon the wondering multitude,
His calm, clear accents fell.

"Romans!" he said, "not arms, not wealth
Heaven claims of you this day;
Nor gifts of wisdom, love or lore,
Howe'er so precious they.

"Hear me, Oh citizens of Rome!
This lesson richly prize;
Best gift and parent of good deeds
Is true *self*-sacrifice.

"I offer to the immortal gods,
Who hark my solemn vow,
That life which for my country lived;
Which dieth for it now."

He backed his steed; threw down his casque
Gazed on the Sacred Height;
Then—forward to the vast abyss
As soldier to the fight.

With right hand raised above his head,
His sword within its sheath,
He urges on the maddened steed
Which bears him to his death.

One moment, and with mighty bound,
He plunges to repose;
One dull, sad sound; but one, and then—
The yawning gulf doth close.

# CRAWFURD CASTLE.

# CRAWFURD CASTLE.

## I.

'Yond many a crimsoned thorn-hedge
In that sweet English vale
Where violet, pink and eglantine
Waft incense on the gale.

Where from the wayside hillocks smile
Gay groups of golden-rod;
And 'neath the shade of branching elm,
The lithe-limbed bluebells nod.

Beneath that lofty, grey stone arch;
Beneath that sculptured crest;
Betwixt those pillars huge, whereon
Heraldic lions rest.

Up through green woods of storied fame;
Where squire with hawk and hound,
And monarch with his glittering train
Had sought a hunting ground.

Unto that gently rising slope;
There Crawfurd Castle stands,
With lordship, far as eye can reach,
O'er all the County lands.

But why, in its kingly grandeur
Of terrace, arch and tower,
Stands that fair structure mute and lone
As hermit in his bower?

*      *      *      *      *

On this same Crawfurd Castle, nigh fourscore years agone,
The morning dawned full cheerily, the sun as brightly shone,
The rooks rehearsed their noisy caw, the lark trilled roundelay
As if this sorrow-freighted world rejoiced in holiday.

Anear the Gothic window, through which the orient beams
Fell in subduèd radiance o'er young life's happy dreams,
Sat one whose noble form and mien, firm step and shapely hand
Proclaimed him born with either right, to serve or to command.

This day was of his happy life, the happiest, brightest far,
For a blissful calm had fallen on a bitter family jar;
The Earl had yielded; on the morn his loved and only son
With full consent would wed with her whose heart had long been won.

She was no child of fortune the lady of his choice;
A lovely face, a faultless form, a clear and kindly voice
Were hers, with wealth of tenderness, and heart of honest love,
Which prized him for his own true worth all other claims above.

She was no peeress of the realm; no high born titled dame,
To lead the dance in glittering halls where myriad jewels flame;
To circle in the slippery round of fashion's giddy throng;
To charm the audience with a sound whence dwells no soul of song.

Yet, brighter to her lover's eyes those coils of golden hair
Than coronet of strawberry leaves, o'ertopped with pearlets rare;
And dearer to her lover's heart those accents sweet and low
Than choicest melody of art, or studied music's flow.

So Viscount Edwin sat and dreamed bright dreams of after hours
When the curate's winsome daughter should reign at Crawfurd towers;
And a new, sweet peace stole o'er him as he thought of all the scorn
With which the Earl had spoken of the maiden lowly born.

How he had pointed to their sires, and reasoned of disgrace,
While bitter disappointment had paled his noble face;
Then how, relenting for the sake of her long since in heaven,
He'd ta'en his boy unto his heart, and seeming wrong forgiven.

Then o'er the dreamer's youthful face there stooped a passing cloud;
But an angel voice made whisper beyond the satin shroud,
As a gentle hand pressed tenderly upon the smooth, white brow,
"I loved thee, Oh my little one!—I love and bless thee now."

## II.

"Dear Cousin Ida! on this day I crave thy special grace!"
The red tide surged in angry force; deep flushed the comely face.
"I may not wish you well," she said, "it cannot come to me
That aught could ever bridge the gulf 'twixt such as her—and thee."

Lord Edwin proffered no reply; she was his childhood's friend;
"Come Fido!" to his faithful hound, "our cheerful way we'll wend
Across the park, adown the mead, on to the river's side
Where, 'neath the jasmine's fragrant shade, the glad hours quickly glide."

Oh! lightly o'er the heart of youth life's scathing breezes blow;
To vanish, as 'fore noonday sun, the first, soft flakes of snow;
And smiles the buoyant hope of youth as smiles the tranquil shore
When Ocean, having spent his wrath, retreats with sullen roar.

At early morn the nuptial peals rang forth full merrily;
Before the lark sang matin song the village stirred with glee;
The agèd church looked young again, in arch and pillar green,
As through the quaint, old diamond panes peeped in the rising sheen.

A joyous crowd hath filled the pews; along the sacred walls,
Even as a benediction, the orient glory falls;
The choir within the chancel sit, the organ swell expands,
The clergyman who baptized both will link the lovers' hands.

Why cometh not the maiden in her crown of orange flowers?
Why linger Earl and bridegroom gay amid their haughty towers?—
Bring hither cypress garnishing! nor bay nor orange bloom;
For music and for marriage-feast are silence and the tomb.

With song and voice of cheering the barque doth hoist her sails,
But who shall tell if into port she'll glide with favouring gales;
The golden chalice of the years with joy may overflow;
Drink whilst ye will the sweetened draught, the end ye may not know.

Upon his couch at morning tide the noble bridegroom lies;
Nor wedding peal will break his rest, nor dawn will ope his eyes;
The violets shall bloom and fade, the river sing its rhyme,
That ear attuned to echoes sweet, is closed to notes of time.

Still robed in richest evening dress, within her tiring-room
The Lady Ida sitteth, but her soul hath passed to doom;
One line to solve the mystery; one only line, which read:
"She wiled from me the living! she cannot part the dead!"

* * * * *

Oh! saddest note in saddening song!
The fair, unwedded bride
With reason fled, might oft be seen
Near by the river side.

Now plaiting wreaths of sweet, wild flowers
To rhythms light and gay;
Now listening for the manly step
She hailed in former day.

Till the Father, in His mercy,
Sent an angel from above
To tend her guileless spirit up
Into the haven of love.

Earl Crawfurd, crushed with shame and woe
Bent low his stately head;
And, ere the forest leaves were strewn,
He slumbered with his dead.

His mansion, with ancestral lands,
Rich farms and pastures fair;
A vast and goodly heritage,
Passed to a distant heir.

So now, in its kingly grandeur
Of terrace, arch and tower,
Stands Crawfurd Castle, mute and lone
As hermit in his bower.

# SONGS OF SCOTIA.

# THE SCOTCH GATHERING.

Hurrah for Scotland's ancient flag!
Now floating on the breeze;
Its every wave in vision paints
A clime beyond the seas.

And, as that music fills the air
Which breathes of mountain-steep,
Our spirits wander back again
To where our fathers sleep.

Again we hear the dashing foam
Which plunges down the dell;
Or ramble o'er the broomy knowes,
Or cull the sweet bluebell.

Or sit in restful gloaming-tide,
'Neath honeysuckle porch,
And watch the tewhits winging low
Beyond the old, grey church,

As balmy breath of briar and thyme
Comes wafted o'er the moor,
And sheds the gold, laburnum fringe
Upon its grassy floor.

Or linger by the martyrs' grave;
Or tread the hallowed sod
Where Hope and Valour stoutly fought
For country and for God.

The Cora Lynn yet sings the dirge
And deeds of Wallace wight;
Whilst Bannockburn still echoes forth
Who bravely died for right.

Oh! beauteous, tender mountain land!
Where'er thy children roam,
Along their lives the heartstrings thrill

To tune of "Home! sweet Home!"

Thy halls of learning grace the earth,
And dignify the name
Which side by side hath ever stood
With honor, truth and fame.

Thy sons, who now with strong, right arm
The stone and hammer wield,
Type well the sires who glory gained,
Or perished on the field.

Now, three cheers for our Highland Chief!
Three more for the Macneill![5]
Three for all those who fondly prize
The land we love *sae weel*!

And three cheers for our noble Queen!
Who from the Bruce descends;
Whose life, attuned to sympathy,
A nation's love defends.

[5] "The Macneill."—Archd. MacNeill, Esq., long the President, and ever an ardent supporter of the Caledonian Club.

# SKYE.

HAIL to the clime of the mist and the mountain!
Of cataract foaming in boisterous glee;
Hail to Cuchullin! proud-peering through cloudland,
In red, rocky grandeur, from sea unto sea.
Fair isle of the patriot, the sage and the songster!
Thou shrine of the deeds of the noble and brave!
Who lived for their kinsmen, who died for their country;
Whose ashes repose in a far, foreign grave.

Of spirit undaunted, of intellect bright
As the glistening lakes in thy bosom which lie;
The archives of learning, the annals of might
Shall lustre for ever the heroes of Skye.[6]
Injustice may scathe thee, deep gloom thee surround,
Thy night shall yet vanish, bright dawn to restore;
When peace and fair plenty once more shall abound,
From Macleod's sea-girt castle to Armadale's shore.

---

[6] "The heroes of Skye."—During the Peninsular war the small island of Skye sent out, to fight the battles of Great Britain, no fewer than ten thousand men, many of whom arose to highest positions in the army.

## "BONNIE DUNDEE."

WHENE'ER I hear the well-kent tune
My heart gangs ower the sea
And communes with the loved o' yore
In the dear auld countrie.

Ance mair I run, wi' lichtsome step
And spirits fu' o' glee
Ane o' a joyous, childish group
To school, in fair Dundee.

Ah! many a year has come and gane
Yet, time's long bridge atween
I overstep, and live the past
As if it happed yestreen.

Though mony a hand is cauld in death,
And mony a grave grows green
O' those that made the Yule-tide bricht
And hanselled Hallowe'en.

But, sometimes from the music creeps
A sicht that blurs the sang;—
'Twould discord sweetest tones e'er sung,
And put the minstrel wrang.

It is the picture o' a hame
O' Scotland's peasantry;
In front stands Graeme of Claverhouse
The *braw* Viscount Dundee.

The troopers rein their panting steeds
Their General's will to bide;
As, clinging to their mother's gown
The frightened bairnies hide.

I hear the haughty "Where is he?"
But—Oh, she answers well!
Her faithful heart love fortified,
"That same I will na tell."

Dark grew his scowl; as fierce wild beast
Defrauded of its prey,
With thirst of blood insatiate,

He gave his passions play.

"Then, woman, thou shalt surely die
Who darest me to my face!"
The husband heard these words of doom
And left his hiding place.

Alack, the courtly cavalier!
*The bonnie, braw* Dundee![7]
What odium of saintly blood
Must ever cling to thee.

He stood his human target up,
He gave the order "Fire!"
Yet, every gun was mute, for ance
His veterans braved his ire.

He raised aloft a coward hand
And shot his victim down;—
But lang in Scotia's heart will live
The memory o' John Brown.

The widowed knelt upon the sward,
Her apron she unbound;
And tenderly, her loved dead
In reddening shroud she wound;

"What think ye o' your husband now?"
The murderer demands
Of the humble woman, in her woe
Clasped firm by bairnies' hands.

She raised the head upon her lap,
She kissed the yet warm brow;
*"I aye thocht muckle o'm,"* she said
*"But mair than ever now."*

Oh, woe for Scotland when her king
Stept 'twixt her and her God!
And baptized in her martyrs' gore
Each cave and moorland sod.

And woe to every servile hand
O' persecution's slaves!
Who load their weakling souls wi' guilt
At beck o' deeper knaves.

Beyond a' creeds and rites o' rule;
True faith shall never fail;
As lighthouse built on solid rock

[7] "Bonnie, braw Dundee."—Graeme of Claverhouse, created for his military services, Viscount Dundee; noted as an able General, but held in detestation as the cruel persecutor of the Scotch Covenanters.

'Twill weather every gale.

And though, unto the powers that be
A loyal lay she'll sing,
Auld Scotland's soul will bend to nane
Save Heaven's own glorious King.

# THE HEATHERBELL.

OLD England wreathes her gorgeous rose
With minstrelsy sublime;
The flower to Highland hearts most dear,
I fain would praise in rhyme.

It bloometh not in palace grounds,
But on the rough hillside;
It boasteth no patrician birth,
It is a people's pride.

Where streamlet leaves its rocky bed
To warble o'er the plain;
Where cataract leaps forth in foam,
On to the seething main.

Down-trampled on the serried field
Where love from love was riven;
Where patriot soul was offered up
As incense unto Heaven.

Where young hearts meet at eventide,
The old, old tale to tell;
In shady nooks, by purling brooks,
There blooms the sweet harebell.

Where cadence of the martyrs' hymn
Bright seraphim revoiced,
As e'en from moorland, fen and cave
Old Scotia's saints rejoiced.

Where ruin mocks those hoary towers
In which mailed knight held sway;
Beside the peaceful cottage door,
Type of this better day.

Bright silvery lochs! dark frowning crags!
Which Scotia's history tell;
Ye impress on my heart of hearts
The land I love so well.

And, through the golden glory-glist
O'er mount, and rock and fell,
There smileth up to Memory's eyes
The dear, Scotch Heatherbell.

# BONNIER.

Oh! bonnie is the tender licht
Within the lovers' een;
But, bonnier a soul that's bricht,
A conscience ever clean.
And braw the form o' manly youth,
Wi' bearing firm and free;
Yet, grander far the lip o' truth,
And heart o' constancy.

Oh! radiant gleam the marble halls
And mausoleums o' pride;
But kindlier the love-licht falls
Around mine ain fireside.
And blithe the merry mavis' sang
Ower copse, an' clover lea;
Yet, cheerier tones I'll lilt ere lang,
Through a' eternity.

# THE DOCTORS FEE.

It was a dazzling equipage
That drove up to the door;
It was a note with lordly crest
The liveried footman bore.
A note for Doctor Harrington
From Lady Cecil Grey;
It told of sickness at the Hall
And begged for no delay.

The young physician pondered
If luck his path had found;
Meanwhile the highly-mettled steeds
Impatient paw the ground.
"'Tis passing strange her ladyship
Though odd, should summon me;"—
High hung the omen of success,
Bright gleamed the golden fee.

Two miles along the country road,
Two miles of avenue
And, 'yond the lily-bordered lake,
Fair turrets rise to view.
Oh! common ills of base-born life
How could ye venture near?
Why should your breath, Oh foul disease!
Pollute such atmosphere?

Deep sadness broodeth o'er the Hall,
Scent-laden breezes sigh,
Though linnets pipe their tuneful song,
And cushat-doves reply.
The menials walk with noiseless tread
Across the French-tiled floor;
And, on its glittering hinges
Swings back the oaken door.

"Oh doctor!" quoth the Lady Grey
With outstretched jeweled hand,
"I am in depths of sore distress
But—you will understand.

It comforts me, that to my wish
The answer came so quick;
See!" and she drew the screen aside;—
*"My favorite cat is sick."*

Well was it that the patient lay
Within a darkened room;
The sunlight on the doctor's face
Had sunk in sudden gloom.
'Twas but a moment; skilled, acute
And witty too, withal,
With sober and respectful mien
He kept his thoughts in thrall.

What were those thoughts? upon that couch
By rarest art compiled,
Lay soulless brute, while o'er the wilds
Strayed many a starving child.
But wealth oft nurseth foibles
To fill its empty day;
And workers cater for its will
Who hope for handsome pay.

With solemn guise he lent his ear
For quite a lengthened space;
Then, with a grave obsequiousness,
He diagnosed the case.
"His stomach is, for sure, deranged;
No appetite hath he;
Yet time and care effect a change,
Wilt thou trust him with me?"

A maiden, on a cushion soft,
The precious tabby bore
To the escutcheoned carriage which
Soon halted as before.
And the doctor raised his patient
And stroked his shiny pate,
Then—in the pantry, 'neath a tub,
Consigned him to his fate.

Withhold thy censure! rude this course
Yet savoring keen insight;
Four days of prison treatment brought
Luxurious Tabby right.
Mote all the victims of excess
Be held in durance vile
A wholesome world would bloom apace,
And peace and plenty smile.

The proverb reads "'Tis an ill wind
That bloweth no one good"
And in the sequel of this tale
Be that fact understood.
For the fancies of a weakling
And over-pampered mind
Were ladders by which highest aim
Could fairer prospect find.

Back came dear Tabby to the Hall
With appetite restored;
Glad to devour the meanest crumb
He hitherto ignored,
To Lady Cecil's wonderment.
With generous courtesy
She poured from out her silken purse
The shining golden fee,

She placed it in the doctor's hand.
"Five hundred pounds a year
As my physician you may claim;" —
She praised him far and near.
He gained the best of patronage
Through all the country side;
He wooed a baron's daughter fair,
And won her for his bride.

No more chagrin, nor vexed delays;
No plodding up the hill;
Life's current flowed as peaceful stream
Which works the well-set mill.
The noble Countess and her cat
Have long since passed away;
But the witty doctor lives and thrives
In green old age this day.

# THE VISION.

I DREAMT that I culled the wild flowers on the moorland,
And roamed o'er the hills which my forefathers trod,
Ere their life-blood empurpled the fields of Hispania;
Ere their souls soared on high to the patriot's God.
I saw, to the call of the pibroch, advancing
O'er mountain, o'er river, o'er blossoming plain,
The strength of strong manhood, the youthful in daring;
The thousands who went, but who came not again.

The many moons passed as a breath, in bright dreamland,
I looked from lone valley to sea-beaten shore;
Two frigates,[8] full-manned with a nation's defenders,
Britannia's proud ensign defiantly bore.
Then up from the shadows came voices long silenced;
"Oh Britain! thou boast of the free and the brave;
We fought, and we died for thy honor, thy freedom,
Thou yieldest our offspring no boon but the grave."

Dark visions rolled off with the mists of the morning;
High o'er the green larches white smoke-wreaths had curled;
And the tender sun beaming from out the clear ether,
Was the hopefuller sun of an opening world.
And over wide ocean a warbler came winging,
Who sang, as he dropped a heathbell by our door,
"The shadows are flitting, the day-dawn is breaking,
The long night of sorrow will darken no more."

---

[8] "Two frigates."—When the descendants of many of those brave soldiers lately rebelled against landlord tyranny, warships were despatched to Skye, to intimidate the oppressed.

## LOCH KATRINE.

Loch Katrine's bonnie banks an' braes,
Though lang I've left them a', laddie,
'Thochts o' them, an' ither days
Maist break my heart in twa, laddie.
Fu' thretty years o' storm an' shine
Sin' first we crossed the ocean's brine,
Yet closely roond oor hearts entwine
The mem'ries o' lang syne, laddie.

Oh! mind ye o' the leafy bowers
Within the sylvan shade, laddie,
Where aft we pu'd the wild-wood flowers,
As warblers stirred the glade, laddie?
Wi' step sae buoyant, firm an' free
I hurried tae the trystin' tree;—
Sae sacred then tae Love an' thee;
To love, an' thee, an' me, laddie.

In school, at sport, in whirlin' dance,
Thy rival was nae seen, laddie,
Nae ither suitor won a glance
Frae me, the village queen, laddie.
Then ebon was my glossy hair,
Thy crown o' curls was gowden fair;
Now time—wha rich nor puir will spare—
Has bleached oor locks to sna, laddie.

Nae mair upon auld Scotia's shore
Wi' willing feet we'll stray, laddie,
Nor greet the freens we loved o' yore,
The yore sae far away, laddie.
Nae mair we'll see the sunbeams rest
Upon Ben Ledi's haughty crest,
As, reddening a' the distant west,
Sol sinks aneath the wave, laddie.

Nae mair we'll watch the rushin' tide
Sweep ower the yellow sands, laddie,
But far ayont the ither side
We'll clasp the lang missed hands, laddie.

Yes! far ayont the mist an' rain,
An' days of toil, an' nichts o' pain,
Wide scattered flocks will meet again
Nae mair to part for aye, laddie.

As frost dispels 'fore kindly thaw
When Spring's saft breezes blow, laddie,
So gently may we slip awa'
To joys nae mortals know, laddie.
For as the sun clears aff the dew,
Our withered lives will bloom anew,
When this fause world shall fade frae view
In fairer worlds abune, laddie.

# CONTENT.

In splendour of an Eastern night,
Where Luna softly smiles,
I've sailed along the shimmering tide
Which laves the Classic Isles.
Or led the dance in courtly hall,
'Mid gayest of the throng;
Or listed to rare *artistes* pour
Their witchery of song.
And 'yond the murky Tiber's wave
Have strolled 'neath Pincian shade;
As sunlight streamed o'er Saxon fair,
Or dark-eyed Roman maid.

In dreamland oft our Highland hills
Forth from the shadows spring,
All radiant in their purple bloom;
Meet haunts of forest king.
And up the green-arched avenue,
And o'er the daisied lawn
Troop faces bright, and hearts as light
As step of mountain fawn.
And artless voices drown in mirth
The sighing of the breeze;—
But memory opes, the vision fades;
Wail not *their* fate; Oh Seas!

Though former scenes in Time's rough blast
Have drifted far away;
And halls wherein our fathers ruled
Lie mouldering in decay,
Though ne'er again, o'er heathery wild,
I'll see the storm-clouds fly;
Or watch the golden glory creep
O'er lake, and mount and sky.
Though never more, from castle tower
I'll scan the pebbly shore;
Or hark the lovèd brother's lays
Chime with the plashing oar.

Yet, where no floweret ever fades,
Nor weeping wakes the morn;
Where every heart, with sorrow fraught,
To joy shall be re-born.
Within the great orchestral band
Glad anthems we'll prolong;
Nor sickness shall discord our praise,
Nor death disturb our song.
Nor ocean wide shall e'er divide,
Nor years nor space will sever;
In realm of health's immortal bloom
We'll live in love for ever.

What though my hope-fraught argosy
Ne'er reached a halcyon strand;
Though winds and waves have rudely tossed;
I know the Pilot's hand
Will steer me safe 'yond shifting-sands,
Dense fogs and chilling rime,
To anchorage within that haven,
Beyond the ridge of time.
Where crowns of pearl, and harps of gold
In holy radiance beam;
Where halos from the great White Throne
Dispel earth's fitful dream.

# MISCELLANEOUS.

# COLUMBUS.

Down in the darkness till earth-crust doth part,
Is the gold of the unwrought mine;
Deep in recess of the lowliest heart
Rare diamonds of genius may shine.
And as from its earth-bed pure gold is revealed,
To work out the projects of man,
So promptings of genius, unraveled, unsealed,
Are but links in eternity's plan.

Onward, aye on o'er the fathomless brine,
From the far Castilian land;
'Neath an ardent sun, 'neath a pale moonshine,
With prow to the halcyon strand.
On from the jeers of a skeptical crowd
To the goal of his long life dream;
On, on from the taunts of the wisdom-proud
To the summit of vast brain scheme.

On with the aid of a womanly wit,
Which served the high-set purpose well;
For the squadron's glittering sails were lit
Through fair Hispania's Isabel.
Who had stooped her head, with its regal crown,
And soothed with pity's shapely hand,
As to grim Suspicion's withering frown
She raised the sceptre of the land.

Onward, aye on, though the night shadows lower,
Though star lamps burn low in the sky,
Onward through hurricane, cloud-rift and shower;
Still onward, whate'er may defy.
Calming, controlling a mutinous crew,
The victims of loneness and fear;
Deftly explaining phenomena new
With voicings of courage and cheer.

Shifting of compass, strange lights in the sky,
Strange birds on a wandering wing;
"On, Oh my comrades! the guerdon is nigh;
Fresh life to my pulses doth spring.
Trust me, my comrades! nor wild water-wraith,
Nor phantom his passage e'er bars
Whose rudder is set with a firm-bound faith
In that Power who created the stars."

On through the drift-weed; Lo! tranquil blue seas;
With breath of a balmier air;
On, hoisting their sails to the landward breeze,
On, ridding their spirits of care.
Light through the darkness! bright beacons ahead!
And the mariner's sails are furled,
For the errand of genius hath aptly sped,
On the rim of a great New World.

In raiment of splendor the ground he hath trod;
He looks from the sky to the main;
He planteth the Cross in the name of his God,
His standard in token of Spain.
And on through the cycles, in Temple of Fame,
Though nations and systems decay,
The laurels which lustre Columbus' proud name
In freshness shall blossom for aye.

## TIME AND ETERNITY.

Time! Ocean of boundless unrest!
Upheaving with tumult of life;
While, as foam on the billowy crest,
Floats he who is first in the strife.
First in the van of courage and right,
Or foremost in daring to wrong;
Time bendeth low to the monarch of might,
Embalms him in story and song.

Yet lives there be which the giddy hours
Tinge lightly, as onward they wing;
Rough winds may scatter Hope's fairest flowers,
The dreamer awaketh to sing.
And sweet seraph tones, borne from on high,
Enliven the faltering strain;
Till a golden rift streaks the dark sky,
And sunlight illumines again.

Eternity! prospect sublime!
Blessed Faith holdeth forth unto view,
Where the fleeting illusions of time
Yield place to the lasting and true,
Where the song never dies in a wail,
Nor sun ever sinks into gloom;
Nor bright life in its splendor doth fail
'Fore darkness of death and the tomb.

When the glare and the glitter shall wane
In glow of the chrysolite sea,
For leal hearts that now struggle in vain
Shall the crown of the victor be.
And sorrow-dimmed lives shall relight
With warmth from an heavenly ray;
And flowerets nipped by an early blight
Shall re-bloom through an endless day.

# THE TREE.

## WRITTEN FOR ARBOR DAY.

THOU! noblest of all nature's growth!
Where'er thy foliage falls,
Thy beauty, wed to matchless worth
The willing heart enthralls.

Erst-while the Jewish exiles hung
Their harps thy boughs along
And poured their wearied spirits forth
In strains of plaintive song.

So yet, 'neath shimmer of thy leaves
Roll back the waves of time,
And exiled souls, in dreams return
To far, serener clime.

Before the German peasant's eyes
Thuringian forests bloom;
Whilst ilex of the sunny South
Lights up Italia's gloom.

The English hail their country's oak,
Through which great victories came;
Since naval power, in danger's hour
Sustained old England's fame.

The ebon cross of Erin's Isle
Bedecks her loyal daughters,
In every land, on every strand
Laved by the glittering waters.

Ah! sweetly 'mong the rowan-trees
Ayond the seething brine,
The Scotsman hears loved melodies,
From voices o' langsyne.

A landmark thou in vale of years!
White stone in history!
Loud publisher of private wrongs,
Or nation's victory.

'Neath agèd oak of Elderslie
Five centuries tell the tale
How, at the name of Scotland's Chief
Her enemies turned pale.

An English yew-tree speaks her fate
Who, by a despot's breath
In brilliant beauty graced a throne,
Then sank in shameful death.

Trees note the spot where Bonaparte
Surrendered at Sedan
Ambition's sceptre, framed of guilt
In blood of brother man.

Whilst ever, through the cycling years,
Judea's olive tree
Proclaims the sin-fought conflict gained
On dark Gethsemane.

By soul, that in the greening leaf,
The Great Designer sees,
Sweet whispers from the Living Life
Are heard among the trees.

And every changing summer hue
Which decks the forest band
Low bends in homage grateful hearts
To Him whose faultless hand

Doth sap the seed, and sun the stem,
And rear the structure high;
Till emerald censers incense waft
Through fair, cerulean sky.

Whose artist-touch illumes the doole
Of woodland's waning green,
With flashing streaks of red and gold,
Sunlit of glorious sheen.

So Faith may gaze, with restful eye,
Across this desert wold;
To find the darksome shades of earth
Relieved by Heaven's bright gold.

So Hope may realize that day,
Beside the crystal river,
Where, sheltered by the Tree of Life,
Pure joys flow on forever.

# THE SHIPWRECK.

Thou! glorious, pure, unwavering Light!
Let not our light be vain!
Grant us to see, through densest night,
Earth's direst problems plain!

A ship held fast on a treacherous reef
Lies quivering to and fro;
The wild winds mocking man's relief;
Upheaving ocean's flow.

Bright crimson floods the burnished west,
Red glows the village spire;
And the darkening speck, on seething crest,
Low sinks in molten fire.

Ah me! amid the tangled heap
Cast forth ere morning chime,
The veteran in his unrocked sleep;
Fair youth, and manhood's prime.

What treasure lieth, tightly bound
Within that sodden vest?
Which rude sea-wave hath not unwound
From off the quiet breast.

"Is't gold or pearls? grim sailor, speak!
What doth that case conceal?"
But the tear adown the bronzèd cheek
All silently doth steal.

They pass it round with reverend grace;—
Only a picture fair;
A woman's, and a baby's face,
And two damp locks of hair.

'Neath peaceful shades they calmly sleep
Who fought the angry wave;
Nor maid, nor mother e'er shall weep
Beside her sailor's grave.

For the golden locks will dull to dark,
The brown will turn to grey;
But the brave who sailed in that gallant bark
Have bade "Farewell" for aye.

# DE PROFUNDIS.

I LOOKED abroad; gloom, only gloom;
Weird, solemn, chill and densely drear;
Black curtain over nature's bier;
Silence oppressive as of doom.

"Oh soul!" I said, "though morn be bright,
Though gorgeous vistas charm life's day,
Descends on every earth-trod way
Cold mortal chill, bereavement's night."

Once more I looked; transcendent shine!
The myriad gates of light unbarred;
The glowing heavens serenely starred;
Dull earth transformed to scene divine.

Then said I, "Soul! would the mercy beams
Shed ever such radiant light,
Had'st thou not known dark sorrow's night
Or groped within this world of dreams?"

# THE ECLIPSE OF THE MOON.

**NOVEMBER 15TH, 1891.**

In her calm, tender, beauty arising
She smiled as she journeyed on high;
Till the shadows fled far o'er the pineland,
Till ocean smiled back to the sky.
And our souls, in those genial rays basking,
Which glorified river and shore,
Soared high from the loved of the life that is,
To the loved of the life evermore.

But lo! o'er the brightness, and beauty and grace
Creeps slowly a dismal, black screen;
Now veiled from our eyes is the centre of light,
Earth's shadows have fallen between.
A moment obscure, then a clear shining rim,
As gleam of the covenant bow;
The veil is withdrawn from fair Luna's bright face,
And the heavens are again in a glow.

Thus basketh the soul in that holier light
Which beameth from Centre Divine;
Thus veiled is the radiance uplifting the life
When we kneel at a worldly shrine.
Yet steadfast and clear is that earth-clouded Light
The penitent, looking on high,
Will view the dark curtain to density glide,
And mercy re-lighten the sky.

# ERIN'S ADDRESS TO FREEDOM.

## VS. LANDLORDISM.

Thou Freedom! which in years agone
Sat gloriously upon our hills;
Through all these verdant valleys shone,
And sang in all those mountain rills.

Oh Thou! for whom my children fought;
Their blood upon thine altar stands;
The sacrifice! was it for nought?
Is it for nought *these* clasp their hands?

Their wills were iron—not their lungs;—
They shrank not from the fiercest fight;
Their deeds, more than ten thousand tongues,
Plead loudly for their offsprings' right.

Oh! what to us that golden age
When Athens reigned, or ancient Rome;
We need not grope through history's page
To greet the scourge we find at home.

My leal ones crave no wizard wand
With topaz gleams their path to pave;
But justice, freedom, fatherland,
A hopeful life, and peaceful grave.

Obedient ever to those laws
Which jar not with that Higher Will;
Thou! Leader in their righteous cause,
With beacon rays their spirits fill.

Thou mayst not see—for Falsehood veils,
And Truth retires when tyrants reign—
Those scenes 'fore which all nature pales,
Nor list the cry of hunger-pain.

Yet thee we hear in every breeze
That round the lonely hamlet raves;
Thy mountains echo to thy seas—
"Ye sons of freemen be not slaves."

Before Despair's dim, hollow eye,
Starvation's wan and wasted cheek,
Can soul of man stand idly by?
God of their fathers, aid the weak!

Through centuries of direst gloom
The Afric prayed thy dawn to see;
At length there tolled Oppression's doom
Out-rung with notes of jubilee.

Too long, in Sorrow's dusky shroud
Thy glorious mien is hid from view;
Now Courage wakes, and calls aloud,
Come forth! thou birthright of the true!

And Thou shalt come! for plaintive song
In minor tone, on bended knee,
Shall rise the power to conquer wrong;—
And Erin's Ireland shall be free.

# THE GIFT.

A BASKET of beautiful roses!
Snowflakes in a setting of green;
Pure as the pearl that reposes
On breast of the daintiest queen.
Not one, but a wealth of sweet roses!
In vases, on table and chair,
Small hands, in haste have deposed them;—
Sweet incense in soft summer air.

*   *   *   *   *

Long faded, Oh friend! are the roses;
Long faded, and fallen away;
But the fragrance such bounty discloses
Doth perfume the wintriest day.
Fragrant as breath of thy roses
Thy life-deeds are wafted above;—
Short season of struggle and triumph!
Bright crown of ne'er withering love.

## EVER FAITHFUL.

SINCE thy dear love my life hath blessed,
Since thy true heart is heart of mine,
Naught fearing, I shall bide the rest;
Though sunlight dim to taper-shine.

Though Time's impress hath marked thy brow,
And silver-streaked thy sunny hair;
As autumn winds, before the snow
Of winter, blight the foliage fair,

Yet shall I love thee till the beam
Of lingering soul-light homeward hies;
Then, where sweet zephyrs fan the stream,
Where day's bright glory never dies,

Sunned of those ever hallowing rays;
As endless cycles onward move,
With glad triumph we'll join to praise
The Centre of unfathomed love.

# "ONLY OUR HIRED BOY."

## I.

God-beams of mercy, gleam through the dull haze;
Sunlight and soften the dark rocky ways!

Harmony pealeth o'er mountain and plain;
Alien sin-nature chimes not in refrain.

That holier season was nigh at hand
When the sympathies of the soul expand.

From the warmth and light of the fireside glow
I walked abroad o'er the glistening snow.

When a black cloud over my pathway set;
It loometh before my memory yet.

No hearse, no mourners, no tolling of bells
The one sure fate of humanity tells.

A rough-fashioned sleigh with its motley load,
Glideth quickly over the churchyard road.

The rude pine coffin is set on a stone;
Hastily earth from its earth-bed is thrown.

Lowered the dead; heavy shovels ply fast;
A few brief moments—the vision hath passed.

Nought of lamenting; no vestige of woe;
Just a dark heap, a foul blot on the snow.

Entering the gateway, I reasoned why?
Questioned the scene with a tear-bedimmed eye.

"Only our hired boy!" He carelessly turned;
My innermost soul in my bosom burned.

## II.

"Only your hired boy! yet nurtured in wealth,
Gifted of beauty, and glowing with health.

"Sunned in the rays of an era sublime,
Lulled in the lap of a Christian clime.

"Suddenly fatherless, suddenly poor;
Brave mother-hands keeping want from the door.

"Oh! how the widowed heart clung to that child,
Her one bright star on the darkening wild.

"Welded in sorrow, bereavement and pain;
Time nor eternity severeth twain.

"Hard for new toilers, though strong be the will;
Weary the way up the steep, rugged hill.

"Friendship in fortune is hollow at best;
Sunset of splendor, illuming the west,

"Sinketh unseen 'fore the blackness of night,—
Her spirit reached forth to the land of light;

"She folded her boy to her aching heart,
And you—you promised to do your part.

"With a calm, sweet smile on her lips she died,
And you drew the child from his mother's side.

"Oh! well for him had he sunk to his rest,
Pillowed in peace on that motionless breast.

"Far better his fate had his young eyes closed,
Mantled in shroud where his mother reposed.

## III.

"You took him home. Ah what record of shame!
To the falsity of a home in name.

"Oh stony heart! hard as his frozen bed;
Cold as the snow-drifts which sweep o'er his head.

"Your baby secure, in infancy blessed;
Warm-cradled as bird in the parent nest.

"Your elder boys safe as lambs in the fold;
That mother's loved one left out in the cold.

"Chilled by the coldest of winter's cold days;
Fevered by heat of the sun's hottest rays.

"Lodged in an outhouse, exposed to the sky;
Beasts underneath in a shelter all dry.

"Rest for the horses, but work for the slave;—
Tyrant! thy betters were death and the grave.

"Sick—yes! he told you with faltering breath;
Lazy you termed it, you beat him in death.

"Bridge you the river he crossed to atone?
Drown you with orgies the orphan's sad moan?

"Nay! for those wailings will ring in your ear;
Haunt your night visions, and follow your bier.

"Whilst that mighty Power which hath mother-love given
Will surely unite what asunder is riven.

"And fill with choice music the one silent tone,
By yielding to mother-love all of its own."

## IV.

Ponder life's teachings; con each of them well;
Man, made in God's image, should earth be a hell?

Where were the justice if earth were our all!
Where, if life's limits were girt of the pall!

God of the fatherless! heard'st Thou that cry!
Wail of the orphan-soul piercing the sky.

Yes! Thou didst hear it; that bitter cold night
When the ground was crisp with its coat of white.

Thou sentest Thy angels to bear him away
From his storm-beaten garb of fragile clay.

Tired-out, aching limbs! weary frozen feet!
Ceaseless, toilsome toil! rest—Ah sweet! how sweet!

No mourner knelt down by that lowly bed;
No kindly hand pillowed that dying head.

Nought, save the starlights of loftier space
Beamed tenderly over that still, pale face.

What matter! the billows may rage and foam,
The heaven-bound soul will reach its home.

What matter! the sorrows of earth are o'er;
He hath landed safe on love's native shore.

Where glory-lit mansions resound with joy;
For the mother who lost, hath found her boy.

And glad Hallelujahs bright seraphim sing;
For the once hired boy is a crownèd king.

# LAURELS.

Wreaths for the warrior brave!
He conquered in the fight,
Bright day chased sable night,
Wave banners! proudly wave!

Laurels for statesman bold!
Men wake from callous sleep,
As tones, in pathos deep,
A people's wrongs unfold.

Sweet flowers with poesy chime;—
Gay-deck those poet lays
Which incense care-worn ways,
Raise souls to heights sublime.

Rare flowers of spotless hue
For heralds of the cross,
Who fear nor shame nor loss,
But type the Christ-life true.

Richest of nature's gems
Within His courts we bring;
Ours, and all nature's King;
King of heaven's diadems.

Chaplets for brow of toil!
Rough hands, but heart all rich,
Who fitly fills his niche
On God's life-giving soil.

Flowers for the suffering throng!
Oh meek! long-during band!
High in the painless land
Sad plaint will rise to song.

White-wreathe we infant tombs!
Where breathes no chilling blast,
Where skies ne'er over cast,
Hope's full fruition blooms.

Be-crown the aged heads
With sprays of evergreen!
Earth waneth, heaven serene

Undying lustre sheds.

Bright-fringe, Oh fragrant flowers!
Life's ever-changeful day;
Till shadow's flit for aye,
In amaranthine bowers.

## ST. PATRICK'S DAY.

THE standard of Erin! unfurl it on high!
To greet the bright day which her children hold dear;
Gay joy-bells of gladness ring out to the sky!
Ring out for the Patron, the Saint, and the Seer.

Whose blessed advent woke from the dole of the grave
The nation long shrouded in paganish gloom;
As with tidings of Him who suffered to save,
He pointed to life beyond death and the tomb.

This day the exile retraceth wide ocean,
To rest for a space in his far native land;
Whilst minstrel-soul, tunèd to deepest devotion,
Doth chime in the music which beats on that strand.

Though tuneless the harp that rich melody poured
On the whispering zephyrs which fan thy clear streams,
And voiceless the halls where thy orators soared,
In fancy full flushed with ne'er realized dreams.

Though silence reigns drear o'er Killarney's sweet lakes,
And dark cloudlets brood over loved Arranmore;
Though wave of Loch Neagh in murmuring breaks
And dashes in foam on a desolate shore,

Yet, Erin! thy glory, long prisoned in night,
Will rise to shine forth in effulgence again;
And Hope's rich fruition will bask in the light
Of splendor illuming each mountain and plain.

Thy shamrock may droop by thy clear sparkling fountains,
It bloometh anew o'er this far western wave;
The spirit which rose[9] 'mid the wild Kerry mountains
Yet lives in the soul of thy loyal and brave.

Not by untoward plots, or feats of the sword,
Shall thy stainless honor and truth be maintained;
By purpose of right, and with help of the Lord
Shall the fondest wish of thy leal hearts be gained.

Then mourn not the ages of sorrow and wrong,
But aye keep thy future of blessing in view;

[9] "The spirit which rose."—Daniel O'Connell, the Irish Liberator.

Sad weeping shall merge into triumph's glad song;—
To God, to thy sires, and to Erin prove true.

# TO THE POET.

## I.

Ho, poet of the soul refined!
The muse within that soul enshrined,
Think'st thou to mould unto thy mind
Base, common clay?

Within the church—most holy place—
Endowed of Heaven's especial grace,
The weeds of evil grow apace,
Why not without?

## II.

And yet—tis passing sad that rhyme,
Most fitting garb for theme sublime,
Should trumpet, in high sounding chime,
The thoughts of wrong.

With eagle flights all may not soar,
Nor bask in fields of richest lore,
Yet, poesy a balm should pour
O'er worldly woes.

## III.

Earth's glamour fails, it cannot mar
The calm, pure radiance of the star;
Discordant music floats afar
From real song.

Essence divine! leal hearts will sing
Though baser souls mean offerings bring;
True anthems o'er the false shall ring
Eternally.

# TO THE OCEAN.

MIRROR of might and of splendor!
Type of immensity!
Smiling in face of the upper blue;
Beautiful! crystal Sea!
Yet, under thy brilliant beaming,
As chills at the heart of love
When a smile o'er-gilds the placid face,
Cold under-currents move.

Over thy glistering waters,
Out of the purple haze,
Thrilleth the chords of memory
With touch of other days.
Once more, by thy rim, bright Ocean!
A youthful, happy band
We course along the yellow sands
Afar, in fair Scotland.

Once more we plash our childish feet
Amid thy shining waves;
Or shelter from the sudden gust
Within thy border caves.
Ho! voices of the summer sea!
Ho! voices sweet and low!
Ye mournful chant their requiem,
Those days of long ago.

He sailed upon thy whitened crest,
The choicest of our band;
Thy seething surges wail his dirge
On far New Holland strand.
That other sleeps—we know not where,
Who early braved thy tide;—
Sing wavelets! we shall meet at length
Upon that further side.

Yes, mighty Ocean! all thy storms
Shall lull to perfect peace;
And all thy weary monotones,
With rhythms sad shall cease.

So now, we stand upon thy brink;
Whilst 'yond thy sparkling foam,
We hear sweet voices calling us
To our eternal home.

## "I GAVE HIM AN ORANGE."

### FROM DR. CONROY'S EVIDENCE.

Beside the lowly couch of pain,
They watched the flickering breath;
They knew that mortal skill was vain
To stem the tide of death.

For ruthless hands, and heart impure,
Though unprovoked by strife,
Had aimed the missive all too sure
Which dulled the warm young life.

When skill had failed, love took its place;
The little gift was given;
One moment's brightness lit the face,
And life from death seemed riven.

Oh! deep within each mother's soul
This deed of love shall tell;
While He who made the wounded whole,
Such acts He noteth well.

Yea, Who the reins of right doth hold
'Yond tortuous frauds of time,
Sees brazen vice, ungilt by gold,
And poverty no crime.

He shall adjudge in righteousness,
And sickness, woe and dearth,
With mammon fall; and Heaven's own bliss
Outweigh the wrongs of earth.

# ST. ANDREW'S DAY.

## WRITTEN FOR THE CALEDONIAN CLUB.

ANOTHER year hath passed away!
Once more, a joyous band,
We hail with mirth thy Natal Day,
Saint of the Heather Land.

For, though we love our Island home,
Our "home upon the wave,"
In Fancy's flights those shores we roam
Which Scotia's waters lave.

True Scottish hearts, in every clime,
This day lift up their voice;
And Memory's joy-bells sweetly chime,
And wearied souls rejoice,

As gorgeously, to longing eyes,
Comes forth, in glory bright,
Those mountains which the nearing skies
O'er-flood with purple light.

Again we climb Ben Ledi's steep,
Or skim Loch Lomond's tide;
Or muse where sunbeams softly creep
Through haunts of byegone pride.

Again we tread the Solway shore,
Or banks of bonnie Dee;
Or watch the Forth's proud waters pour
Into the Northern Sea.

Or gaze upon that tragic field
Which ancient minstrel sang;
Where warrior died upon his shield
As shouts of battle rang.

Or hark through Bothwell's ivied towers
Soft winds sonatas play;
Whilst Clutha, sparkling 'yond the bowers
Lights youth's long, golden day.

Fair land! beyond all other lands
The theme of tale and song;
The present and the past clasp hands
Thy glory to prolong.

Disgrace be his, and lasting shame
Who heeds not Heaven's just laws;
And, traitor to the Scottish name
Who owns not freedom's cause.

But hallowed be their memory
Who kept thy honor bright;
Thy great of every century,
Even down to Wallace wight.

*     *     *     *     *

Now drink we to the heath-clad hills
Beloved of bard and sage;
The silvery lochs, the rippling rills,
The blood-bought heritage!

And drink we too, with heart of grace,
Victoria the Good!
Our queenly queen of Stuart race,
That reigned in Holyrood.

All honor to our Highland Chief!
White-wreathed of glory's crown;
Who dignifieth honors brief[10]
His sun shall ne'er go down.

And last we honor each and all
Of Celt, or Saxon blood;
Whose acts attest, in hut or hall
God's type of brotherhood.

---

[10] "Who dignifieth, etc."—Hon. Senator A. A. Macdonald, for some time Member of the Legislative Council, and one of the delegates to the Quebec Conference anent Confederation. Elevated to the position of Lieutenant-Governor of Prince Edward Island, 1884; since, in 1891, appointed to the Senatorship. For the last fifteen years the honoured Chief of the Caledonian Club.

# GOOD-BYE AND GOOD-NIGHT.

Good-bye! it quivers through the years,
Low-breathing of despair;
The sunniest flower of life it sears,
And dulls the summer air.

It echoes through the falling leaves,
Through ocean's ebb and flow;
In Spring's soft gales, in Autumn sheaves;
Sore parting, bitter woe.

It speaketh through the vacant chair
To every yearning heart;
Howe'er so noble, gifted, fair,
Earth-born on earth must part.

Good-night! Oh eyes long used to weep!
Faith spans the mist of years;
High o'er life's toil, death's darksome sleep,
Heaven's fair, sweet dawn appears.

Refulgent with its glorious rays,
O'er earth, o'er ocean's foam;
Where'er the weary wanderer strays,
To light the spirit home.

Home to the painless, sinless land,
The never darkening sky;
Where hearts ne'er break with clasp of hand;
Where friends ne'er say Good-bye.

## THE ROSE.

She passed as a ray of sunshine
O'er the dark, piazza floor;
And the gloaming turned to noonday
As she neared the open door,
And in her white and dainty hands
A precious gift she bore.

Thou baby rose! from parent stem
Far traveller from my heart's first shrine;
Sweet breathings of the olden days
Speak from each tiny leaf of thine;
Thou! velvet-clad in robes of state;
Rich-crimsoned of the Hand Divine.

Sweet art thou as the dreams of youth
Or dew-drops glist 'neath orient ray;
Still, smiling in thy fair, young bloom
Thou'rt frail and perishing as they;
Yet, aftermath of glory-light
Doth rise o'er darkness and decay.

# HOME FROM SCHOOL.

OH! sweet the whispers of the Spring
Which stir the greening leaves;
And sweet the melodies which ring
Through Autumn's golden sheaves.
Oh! sweet the prattle of the rill
As, in its youthful pride,
It danceth down the smiling hill
To join the foaming tide.

But, sweeter far than nature's chime
Unto a mother's ear;
More tender than the river's rhyme
Those tones she longs to hear.
Those notes unset to music's rule;
Those high-strung notes of joy,
Which herald coming home from school;
The coming of her boy.

Oh! beauteous are the rainbow hues
Which deck the oriole's wing;
And sparkling bright the pearly dews
Which 'round fair morning cling.
Oh! lovely are the flowers which wreathe
Heaven's hope o'er earth's dark wold;
And grander far than aught beneath,
Those orbs of gleaming gold.

But, unto mother-love aye true,
More bright than amber sky
That boyish form against the blue,
With ensign cap swung high.
The beauty of that fair young face
Outshines heaven's clearest star;
Nor ills of time will blur its grace,
Nor fate impress one scar.

The waning year is nigh its round,
The air is crisp and cool;
Though footsteps linger, love, unbound,
Doth greet my boys from school.

I feel the shadows lengthening,
The twilight slipping fast;
Yet, through the good God strengthening,
Dark night is soon o'erpast.

Methinks, even in that holier land,
I'll cross the pearly floor,
And by the blessed angel stand
Who guards the hallowed door.
And, while seraphic voices soar,
Amid supremest joys,
From earth's hard school, I'll list once more
To welcome home my boys.

# TO H. M. S. BLAKE.[11]

Hail to Britannia's noble ship!
Whose pendant, streaming high
Doth shadow forth a nation's might
Athwart our placid sky.

Thou comest not in pomp of power,
Nor din of battle's roar;
Thy cannon wake no trembling hearts
Upon our peaceful shore.

Hail to Britannia's sailor sons!
Great sons of greatest fleet!
We tender ye a welcome true
Unto fair Abegweit.[12]

Our happy hearths, our blooming fields
We owe to such as you;
For Nelson, Howard, Frobisher
Were of the "boys in blue."

Long live our noble Admiral!
May his noble deeds afford
That crown which lustres poortith's brow,
And graceth prince or lord.

May bonds of sympathy unite
Great Neptune's greatest sons
With lowliest tar, within whose veins
The blood of fealty runs.

And ne'er forget, on whiche'er sea
The tide of time sweeps past,
*Port La Joie*[13] prays you, 'yond all storm
Safe anchorage at last.

---

[11] "H. M. S. Blake."—H. M. S. Blake, Admiral Sir John Hopkins, anchored in Charlottetown Harbour, 18th August, 1893.

[12] "Abegweit."—Home on the Wave—Indian name for P. E. Island.

[13] "Port La Joie."—Former name of Charlottetown.

# RETROSPECT.

## I

SIR RONALD leaned back in his easy chair;
He gazed abroad on the prospect fair.

On the soft, white carpet of new-fallen snow;
On the ermined branch with its gems aglow.

Snow white those locks of the threescore and ten
Yet, smooth is that brow as of younger men.

He beareth his years with a right good will,
And life floweth on as a placid rill.

For though evening's sun is well nigh set
His heart holds the dawn of the morning yet.

From memory's treasures of years gone by
He portrayed scenes for the mental eye,

Wondrous experience by land and by sea;
Fain would I tell as he told it to me.

## II.

"Drifting of smoke wreath, darting of flame;
The fire-fiend is working his way;
And the ghastly glare o'er the gates of dawn,
Streaks far on the opening day.
The stairway has fallen, the rafters yield,
The flooring is creaking o'erhead;
Yet the stout stone wall as a sentry stands,
Though the surges of battle outspread.

"But lo! from the casement, wide open thrown,
By loving hands carefully bound,
A basket live-freighted is hastily launched
Through flashes of flame to the ground.
Kindled is courage, strong effort revives,
Grim death and destruction are braved;—
What matter the crash of that falling roof!
Dear life, in its lustre is saved."

### III.

"Deep murmurs from out of the frowning skies;
A rising and swelling of seas;
The sailor quick-furleth the outspread sail,
For a hurricane toppeth the breeze.
No shapelier craft from a British port
Ever ventured the heaving tide;
Her firm knit hull, and her rigging taut
Were the mariner's honest pride.

"But what recketh Ocean for pride of man!
The storm-wraith wails loudly on high;
Till battered and torn is the gallant bark
In her wrestle 'gainst ocean and sky.
Yet she conquers, she rideth the seething foam;
And, as bird from prison bars free,
She spreadeth her sail 'yond the storm-cloud's rim
And skimmeth a tranquil sea."

### IV.

"A young mother sat on a vessel's deck,
A flaxen haired babe on her knee;
And her thoughts went back to the mountain land,
And she sighed for her *ain countrie.*
But the light of love, with the hope of youth
In the true woman's heart burns clear;
Oh! what unto her is the loneliest wild
When the arm which she leans on is near!

"One glance to the stalwart form by her side,
Her spirit returns to its rest;
And gaily she dreameth of happier days
In the new land, the glorious West.
She raiseth the babe; Oh well for her peace!
Where had nestled the darling head,
A fierce, flying ball from the Gascon grazed,
Ere it plunged in its ocean bed."

### V.

"Name it not chance; No! in earliest youth
'Twixt the fire, 'twixt the foe and the flood,
Who feedeth the ravens, Who telleth the stars
In the pathway of danger stood.
And, aye and anon, on the journey up hill,
White milestones have pointed the way
Through the tangled maze, o'er the rocky steep,

To the ridge of an endless day.

"Now peaceful in shades of the gloaming I rest,
Unawed of the murkier night;
Calm-souled I await for the upward call,
And the glow of the nearing light.
The river's sad moanings I may not hear;
High over the murmuring foam
Floateth rich music. Ah! sweet to mine ear
Those angel tones welcoming home."

## VI.

Intently I listened, but scant my reply;
Sorrow and gladness o'er-misted the eye.

Gladness for light of a long, lustrous day;
Sorrow for sunshine fast fleeting away.

More dense than the doole of a starless night
The gloom of a soul which knoweth no light.

Down-coursing as cataract o'er the steep hill
That will which opposeth the Higher Will.

Unbeauteous is age when it crusts itself round,
Or buries itself in a selfish mound.

But blessèd be those who in soul-growth expand
'Neath the milder beams from the glory-land.

Yea blessèd they be! when the river is passed,
They shall enter the gate with the palms at last.

**FINIS.**

Lector House believes that a society develops through a two-fold approach of continuous learning and adaptation, which is derived from the study of classic literary works spread across the historic timeline of literature records. Therefore, we aim at reviving, repairing and redeveloping all those inaccessible or damaged but historically as well as culturally important literature across subjects so that the future generations may have an opportunity to study and learn from past works to embark upon a journey of creating a better future.

This book is a result of an effort made by Lector House towards making a contribution to the preservation and repair of original ancient works which might hold historical significance to the approach of continuous learning across subjects.

**HAPPY READING & LEARNING!**

LECTOR HOUSE LLP
E-MAIL: info@lectorhouse.com

9 789356 146358

Printed by Libri Plureos GmbH in Hamburg,
Germany